OXFORD STUDENT TEXTS

Series Editor: Steven Croft

The Struggle for Identity in Modern Literature

Edited by Gloria Morris

D1585826

EG51148

OXFORD
UNIVERSITY PRESS

Great Clarendon Street, Oxford OX2 6DP
Oxford University Press is a department of the University of Oxford.
It furthers the University's objective of excellence in research, scholarship,
and education by publishing worldwide in

Oxford   New York

Auckland   Cape Town   Dar es Salaam   Hong Kong   Karachi
Kuala Lumpur   Madrid   Melbourne   Mexico City   Nairobi
New Delhi   Shanghai   Taipei   Toronto

With offices in

Argentina   Austria   Brazil   Chile   Czech Republic   France   Greece
Guatemala   Hungary   Italy   Japan   Poland   Portugal   Singapore
South Korea   Switzerland   Thailand   Turkey   Ukraine   Vietnam

Oxford is a registered trade mark of Oxford University Press
in the UK and in certain other countries

British Library Cataloguing in Publication Data

Data available
ISBN: 978-0-19-832881-0
3 5 7 9 10 8 6 4 2
Typeset in India by TNQ
Printed in China by Printplus

Paper used in the production of this book is a natural, recyclable product made from wood
grown in sustainable forests. The manufacturing process conforms to the environmental
regulations of the country of origin.

The publishers would like to thank the following for permission to reproduce
photographs:

p3: Rex Features/Everett Collection; p10: Corbis/Colin McPherson;
p157: Oxford University Press; p159: Library of Congress;
p169: Rex Features/Sipa Press; p180: Rex Features/Martin McCullough:
p183: Rex Features/Hallmark Ent/Everett; p189: Rex Features/Stuart Clarke;
p199: Corbis/Robbie Jack; p207: Rex Features/Maggie Hardie

Contents

Acknowledgements   v

Foreword   viii

Modern Literature in Context   1
The struggle for identity   1
The twentieth century   2
New voices, new techniques   11

The Struggle for Identity in Modern Literature   15
A Doll's House: Henrik Ibsen   17
The House of Bernarda Alba: Federico García Lorca   19
The Glass Menagerie: Tennessee Williams   24
All My Sons: Arthur Miller   25
The Go-Between: L.P. Hartley   27
The Thought-Fox: Ted Hughes   28
Things Fall Apart: Chinua Achebe   29
The Prisoner: Amiya Rao   32
Song of Lawino: Okot p'Bitek   34
Digging: Seamus Heaney   38
Follower: Seamus Heaney   40
The Early Purges: Seamus Heaney   41
The Joy of Writing: Wislawa Szymborska   42
The French Lieutenant's Woman: John Fowles   43
I Know Why the Caged Bird Sings: Maya Angelou   47
The Female Eunuch: Germaine Greer   49
The Badness Within Him: Susan Hill   51
This Be The Verse: Philip Larkin   54
Woman Work: Maya Angelou   54
The Company of Wolves: Angela Carter   56
Nella Last's War: eds Richard Broad and Suzie Fleming   58
The Color Purple: Alice Walker   59
I Coming Back: Grace Nichols   61
The Handmaid's Tale: Margaret Atwood   62
Beloved: Toni Morrison   65
Making History: Brian Friel   67

An Evil Cradling: Brian Keenan   69
Introduction to *Six Women Poets*: Grace Nichols   71
Captain Corelli's Mandolin: Louis de Bernières   73
Little Red-Cap: Carol Ann Duffy   75
Knowing Me: Benjamin Zephaniah   77
Spies: Michael Frayn   79
Late Spring: Owen Sheers   82
Mr Pip: Lloyd Jones   83

Notes   85

Interpretations   153
Themes and ideas   153
The loss of innocence and rites of passage   154
The family and family relationships   161
Being a woman   167
Being a man   176
Racial identity   184
Writing and being a writer   190
Language, structure and form   198
Critical perspectives   204

Essay Questions   210

Chronology   213

Acknowledgements

We gratefully acknowledge permission to use the following copyright texts in this book.

Chinua Achebe: extract from *Things Fall Apart* (Anchor 1958), reprinted by permission of Pearson Education.

Maya Angelou: extract from *I Know Why the Caged Bird Sings* (Virago, 1969), copyright © Maya Angelou 1969, and renewed 1997 by Maya Angelou, and 'Woman Work' from *And Still I Rise* (Virago, 1986), copyright © Maya Angelou 1978 reprinted by permission of the publishers, Little Brown Book Group Ltd and Random House, Inc.

Margaret Atwood: extract from *The Handmaid's Tale* (Jonathan Cape, 1985), copyright © O.W. Toad Ltd 1985, reprinted by permission of Curtis Brown Group Ltd, London.

Louis de Bernières: extract from *Captain Corelli's Mandolin* (Vintage, 1994), reprinted by permission of The Random House Group Ltd.

Okot p'Bitek: extract from '2: The Woman With Whom I Share My Husband' from *Song of Lawino* (EAEP, 1966), reprinted by permission of East African Educational Publishers Ltd.

Angela Carter: extract from 'The Company of Wolves' in *The Bloody Chamber* (Vintage, 1995), copyright © Angela Carter 1979, reprinted by permission of the author c/o Rogers, Coleridge & White Ltd, 20 Powis Mews, London W11 1JN.

John Fowles: extract from *The French Lieutenant's Woman* (Little Brown, 1969), reprinted by permission of J.R. Fowles Ltd c/o Aitken Alexander Associates.

Michael Frayn: extract from *Spies* (Faber, 2002), copyright © Michael Frayn 2002, reprinted by permission of the publishers, Faber & Faber Ltd.

Brian Friel: extract from *Making History* (Faber, 1989), copyright © Brian Friel 1989, reprinted by permission of the publishers, Faber & Faber Ltd.

Germaine Greer: extract from *The Female Eunuch* (MacGibbon & Kee, 1970), reprinted by permission of Germaine Greer c/o Aitken Alexander Associates.

L.P. Hartley: extract from *The Go-Between* (Hamish Hamilton, 1953), copyright © L.P. Hartley 1953, reprinted by permission of Penguin Books Ltd.

Seamus Heaney: 'Digging', 'Follower', and 'The Early Purges' from *Death of a Naturalist* (Faber, 1966), copyright © Seamus Heaney 1966, reprinted by permission of the publishers, Faber & Faber Ltd.

Susan Hill: extract from 'The Badness Within Him' from *A Bit of Singing and Dancing and Other Stories* (Long Barn Books, 1973), copyright © Susan Hill 1973, reprinted by permission of Sheil Land Associates on behalf of the author.

Ted Hughes: 'The Thought-Fox' from *The Hawk in the Rain* (Faber, 1957), copyright © Ted Hughes 1957, reprinted by permission of the publishers, Faber & Faber Ltd.

Lloyd Jones: extract from *Mr Pip* (John Murray, 2006), copyright © Lloyd Jones 2006, reprinted by permission of the publishers and Lutyens and Rubinstein Literary Agency on behalf of the author.

Brian Keenan: extract from *An Evil Cradling* (Hutchinson, 1992), reprinted by permission of The Random House Group Ltd.

vi

Acknowledgements from Gloria Morris

I should like to thank Steve Croft for his support and guidance and Jan Doorly for her kind and tactful management. Thanks go also to Peter Morris for his encouragement and patience.

Editors

Steven Croft, the series editor, holds degrees from Leeds and Sheffield universities. He has taught at secondary and tertiary level and headed the Department of English and Humanities in a tertiary college. He has 25 years' examining experience at A level and is currently a Principal Examiner for English. He has written several books on teaching English at A level, and his publications for Oxford University Press include *Exploring Literature*, *Success in AQA Language and Literature* and *Exploring Language and Literature*.

Gloria Morris studied English at the University of East Anglia, including American and European literature, and was later awarded a masters' degree at Sheffield Hallam University. After working for some years as an English teacher in secondary schools as well as in a sixth form college, she became Head of English, Communications and Modern Languages in a large tertiary college. She has worked for many years as a Senior Examiner, Moderator and Advisor in AS/A2 English Literature and has written several student books on English literature.

Foreword

Oxford Student Texts have, over a number of years, established a reputation for presenting literary texts to students in both a scholarly and an accessible way. In response to developments in the structure and approach of A level study, several new editions have been published to help students prepare for the changing emphasis and demands of these courses. These editions have been written with a key focus on a specific area of study and contain a range of texts by a wide variety of writers intended to give a flavour of that area and provide contextual linking material that will help students develop their wider reading on a particular period or topic. Each volume in the series consists of four main sections which link together to provide an integrated approach.

The first part provides important background information about the period or thematic area and the factors that played an important part in shaping literary works. This discussion sets the various texts in context and explores some key contextual factors.

This section is followed by the texts themselves. The texts are presented without accompanying notes so that students can engage with them on their own terms without the influence of secondary ideas. To encourage this approach, the Notes are placed in the third section, immediately following the texts. The Notes provide a brief explanation of individual texts to help set them in context and also give explanations of particular words, phrases, images, allusions and so forth, to help students gain a full understanding of the particular text. They also raise questions or highlight particular issues or ideas which are important to consider when arriving at interpretations.

The fourth section, Interpretations, goes on to discuss a range of issues in more detail. This involves an examination of the influence of contextual factors as well as looking at such aspects as language and style, and various critical views or interpretations. A range of activities for students to carry out, together with discussions as to how these might be approached, are integrated into this section.

At the end of each volume there is a selection of Essay Questions, a Chronology and where appropriate a Further Reading list.

We hope you enjoy reading these texts and working with these supporting materials, and wish you every success in your studies.

Steven Croft   *Series Editor*

Modern Literature in Context

The struggle for identity

The struggle for identity is by no means an exclusively 'modern' concern. Writers from as early as Anglo-Saxon times have raised questions about what it is to be human, as opposed to a god or, at the other end of the scale, a beast, as well as what it is to be a writer.

Literary characters over time have struggled with questions such as 'Who am I?' and 'Where and with whom do I belong?' Individuals have felt their uniqueness and questioned their place in society for a multitude of reasons: because of gender and colour most notably, and also because of age, class, race or religion.

The period from the beginning of the twentieth century to the present day is no different, though it has seen an accelerated pace of change and two world wars, as well as other less all-embracing conflicts (notably the Vietnam War, the Falklands and Gulf Wars, and wars in Iraq and Afghanistan). In addition there have been many other significant events, conflicts and developments, for example in the spheres of medicine, travel, technology, computing and telecommunications. The Internet and the World Wide Web have enabled people from widely diverging countries and cultures to communicate and share ideas in a way that has never been available before. We are increasingly interested in the question of who and what we are, and where we belong. We are more aware of our similarities and differences, including issues of race, religion, class/caste, gender and geography.

One of the most significant developments in literature of the modern era has been the growth and development of texts that examine the role of women in a patriarchal society. This is nothing new – ancient Greek tragedies such as *Medea* examine this idea – but the late nineteenth-century play by Henrik Ibsen,

A Doll's House (see page 17), reflects this theme in a most remarkable way, and created such a stir when it was produced in Germany that the lead actress refused to play the role of Nora unless Ibsen revised the ending (which he reluctantly did, making Nora change her mind about leaving her family, to his later regret). His play suggests that each of the characters has been damaged by their relationship with their father. Ibsen, in a comment on the play's significance, said that 'the strongest man [or woman] in the world is he who stands alone' which is clearly the message of the end of the original version of the play – the one that is performed today.

The twentieth century

The dawn of the twentieth century was perceived by many as a momentous, even portentous time. Famously, L.P. Hartley's novel *The Go-Between* (see page 27) presents English society on the cusp of change from the time of solid Victorian values, in a golden era of long, hot summers and idyllic scenes of outdoor life, and looks towards the new world of the early twentieth century. As one century changes into another, so too the hero, Leo, shifts from childhood to adolescence. This is an important theme, which runs throughout modern literature.

Hartley raises questions not only about this rite of passage from childhood through adolescence to adulthood, and the loss of innocence, but also considers issues of class and social hierarchy. The protagonist Leo struggles to understand the protocols of a system which denies Marion the right to marry her lover Ted, who is a farmer, and pairs her with Trimingham, a lord, so as to elevate her family's social status. The novel famously begins: 'The past is a foreign country: they do things differently there', setting up the notion that, in the case of the narrative of the novel, the behaviour and attitudes of previous eras are alien.

In *The Go-Between*, Leo (seen here in the 1970 film version) is
exploited by adults as he moves from childhood to adolescence

Ideas of class and social hierarchy are also examined by E.M.
Forster in *Howards End* (1910), and he also wrote *Maurice*, which
focuses on a homosexual relationship, at a time when issues of
sexuality were treated cautiously and indirectly by other writers,
if at all. The book was published only after the author's death,
an indication of how secretive Forster was about his own
sexuality. The concept of homosexuality as sinful in a religious
context, and an aberration in a biological context, is the basis for
the secrecy of the character of Carlo in *Captain Corelli's
Mandolin* by Louis de Bernières (see page 73). Carlo hides the
truth about his identity and joins the army to be with the people
he loves the most. He writes a 'confession' to be read only after
his death, because of society's condemnation of homosexuality
at the time when the novel is set, during the Second World War.

This recalls E.M. Forster's secrecy about himself. Certainly a time in which homosexuality was punished by the law does seem to belong to 'a foreign country'.

Another notable novel written at the beginning of the twentieth century has had repercussions that resonate even today: Polish-born Joseph Conrad's *Heart of Darkness*, published in 1902. This short novel is set mainly in the African jungle and sees the protagonist Marlow taking a journey in search of Kurtz, who has left his fiancée in a quest to explore the heart of Africa and has become so corrupted that he has induced members of the local tribes to worship him. He is rescued by Marlow but dies on the way home. His dying words relate to his previous experiences; in a famous scene he whispers 'The horror! The horror!', seemingly unable to bear the identity he has taken on, that of a tyrant. The Nigerian writer Chinua Achebe has taken issue with *Heart of Darkness* because he feels that the black inhabitants of the Congo are presented by Conrad as being inferior to white Europeans. Achebe's 1958 novel *Things Fall Apart* (see page 29) was, to some extent, written to present what he sees as an alterative view of the Igbo people and their English colonizers. It too is a tragic tale, which sees the downfall of the hero Okonkwo. His personal struggle to achieve a reputation as a fearless man and to be unlike his father results in yet more fear – fear of being seen to be afraid and of being like the father he despises. The result is his death by suicide and rejection by his tribe, so that he becomes a footnote in a white man's history book.

Another preoccupation of the literature of the early part of the twentieth century was to examine the role of the outsider. Franz Kafka's short novel *Metamorphosis* (1915) takes as its subject a salesman's sudden transformation into a giant insect, robbing him of his identity as the family breadwinner and leading to a situation where he is despised by his family, those he used to support, as vermin. A work by the French philosopher and writer Albert Camus, *L'Etranger* (*The Outsider*), written in 1941, also takes as its subject a man who is in many ways alienated from the rest of society, principally because he hides nothing, including his unemotional attitude towards the death of his mother. When he is tried for killing a man, this is what the jury cannot forgive him for.

The First World War and its aftermath

The First World War (1914–1918), called at the time 'the war to end all wars', had an enormous effect on British society; it was never to be the same again. The previously rigid class barriers crumbled, and women were forced into roles previously taken on by men, who were now absent fighting. Women's roles had to be redefined, and they had to learn to do 'men's jobs'. The war took a heavy toll as so many young men died, leaving the corresponding generation of women without their partners or husbands. The position of women in society began to undergo a huge change, one that would culminate in the middle of the twentieth century with the rise of feminism.

Much poetry written in English at this time posed questions about the existence of war and humanity's role, as well as God's role, in the slaughter it entailed. The works of Siegfried Sassoon and Wilfred Owen in particular are significant.

After the war there began a gradual breakdown of established patterns of social order. This is vividly portrayed in a novel set at this time, *The Remains of The Day* by Kazuo Ishiguro (1989), which examines the role and identity of the butler and ideas of 'service' while also posing questions about class and social hierarchy as well as politics in the years between the two world wars.

In the years following the First World War there developed, among many people, a distrust of supposed authority, and there was a period of revolt against convention, clearly portrayed in *The Great Gatsby* by F. Scott Fitzgerald (1925). This novel examines 1920s American society alongside the story of Gatsby himself. It raises issues of class in a supposedly classless society; the unremarkable James Gatz redefines himself as Jay Gatsby and

5

in so doing invents a glamorous new identity. Throughout the novel he struggles to impose his new self on those who represent 'old money' (well-established, wealthy families) in New England.

Meanwhile in England, the works of D.H. Lawrence promoted freedom and anti-authoritarianism in, for example, *Lady Chatterley's Lover* (written in 1928 and published privately in Florence). This novel was famously the subject of a trial for indecency in 1960, when it was first published in England by Penguin. It features explicit sexual scenes and 'four-letter words', which caused scandal, as did perhaps the fact that the 'lover' of the title is a gamekeeper on the Chatterley estate, in class terms far below his aristocratic lover Constance Chatterley. This is a pairing like that of Marion and Ted in *The Go-Between*, but whereas the latter relationship ends in tragedy, that of Mellors and Constance does not. Lawrence thought that cohesion between the mind and body was crucial in the realization of one's identity, and it is through her experience of passion with Mellors that Constance achieves a sense of wholeness.

Better and more universally available education in England and wider knowledge of the world contributed to the questioning attitude towards many aspects of social and political life that was characteristic of this time. Women sought more freedom and independence.

The Second World War and its aftermath

The Second World War (1939–1945) was the first to cause heavy civilian casualties in Britain – almost a quarter of the total casualties of the war. In the post-war period there was pressure for social change. The 1944 Education Act guaranteed secondary education up to the age of 15 for all, and measures were put in place to create a National Health Service, with a contributory National Insurance scheme to provide individuals with some financial security throughout life. The nationalization of the coal and steel industries and the railways followed, in a Britain that was recovering from damage to its infrastructure and to its social fabric.

In the wider world India gained independence in 1947, marking the beginning of the break-up of the British Empire. Works such as the four novels in *The Raj Quartet*, written between 1965 and 1975 by Paul Scott, chart the decline of British rule in India, and his shorter novel *Staying On* (set after the exodus of many of the British from India at independence) examines issues of identity from the point of view of a couple who have remained behind in India after the granting of independence. John Masters's novel *Bhowani Junction* (1952) has as its protagonist Victoria, an Anglo-Indian engaged to a Sikh, who realizes that marriage to her fiancé will deprive her of her name and hence her identity; after a period in which she has a relationship with a British officer, she decides that her future is with her long-time admirer Patrick, an Anglo-Indian like herself.

Soon after the Second World War tensions between the West and the Soviet bloc, and the increasing dangers posed by the nuclear arms race, polarized the world's politics. 'Cold war' themes were explored in popular fiction through the novels of writers such as Ian Fleming and John le Carré, whose most famous novel is *The Spy Who Came In From The Cold* (1963). Here identities are changed in a bid to outsmart the 'enemy', so that there is a constant struggle to represent oneself as someone else. Political themes are evident in much writing of the time, most notably in George Orwell's *Animal Farm* (1945) and *Nineteen Eighty-Four* (1949), in which he presents a vision of a future world dominated by totalitarianism. Other texts that feature nightmarish visions of societies of the future, although written in quite disparate times, include Aldous Huxley's *Brave New World* (1932), *Lord of The Flies* by William Golding (1954), and *The Handmaid's Tale* by Margaret Atwood (1985, see page 62).

During the 1950s there emerged a new breed of dramatists and novelists, whose radical views and style of literature challenged social norms. One journalist described them as 'the angry young men', or 'angries' for short, as their writing often contained a strong sense of resentment, betrayal and futility.

They focused on the alienation felt by many people in society, often founded in the perception that post-war promises of a 'new world' had not materialized. John Osborne's play *Look Back In Anger* (1956) is probably the best known of the texts produced at this time. Alan Sillitoe's novel *Saturday Night and Sunday Morning* (1958), like Osborne's play, became a successful film in the popular British Realist Cinema tradition, along with Shelagh Delaney's *A Taste of Honey* (also 1958). Delaney's play considers the role and identity of young unmarried women in relation to parents (in this case a feckless mother), lovers (in this case the protagonist becomes pregnant and bears a mixed-race child, with attendant identity issues) and friends (a homosexual young man takes on the role of her protector, despite her mother's condemnation of his sexuality).

The 'angries' had little coherence as a movement, although all seemed to want to assert English or British provincialism. Other notable writers whose work was coming into prominence at this time because of their anti-authority stance include Kingsley Amis and John Wain. John Braine wrote *Room At The Top* (1957) and *Life at The Top* (1962), charting the progress of working-class Joe Lampton and his attempts to raise himself financially and socially by marrying a local factory owner's daughter. Harold Pinter's play *The Caretaker* (1959) also remains a classic.

Few women writers were prominent at this time, but the post-war years did see a significant increase in the number of women writing in all genres, many of whom focused on issues of particular relevance to women. Significantly, the creation of the publishing houses The Women's Press and Virago encouraged new writers as well as promoting reassessment of the work of earlier women writers. Among those reassessed were Charlotte Perkins Gilman, whose short novel *The Yellow Wallpaper* (1892) looks at the isolation of a young mother suffering from post-natal depression, deemed mad by her doctor husband; Jean Rhys, who wrote her first work *The Left Bank and Other Stories* in 1927, but is most famous for *Wide Sargasso Sea* (1966), the story of the early life of an alienated female character in Charlotte Brontë's *Jane Eyre*; and Radclyffe Hall, whose 1928 novel *The Well of Loneliness* has as its main character an only female child, called Stephen by her parents, who falls in love with a woman. More well-known women writers such as Muriel Spark, Doris Lessing and Iris Murdoch have also been featured.

Trends in poetry

The years since the Second World War have also seen a greatly increased in interest in poetry, notably 'The Movement', a term used in 1954 by J.D. Scott, literary editor of *The Spectator* magazine, to refer to mostly English poets whose aim was to avoid what they saw as excessive romanticism in the use of themes and stylistic devices by writers such as Dylan Thomas, and to avoid political or social comment. (Dylan Thomas, the Welsh poet, is most famous as the author of *Under Milk Wood*, a play for voices first recorded by the BBC in 1954.) 'The Movement' poets included Kingsley Amis, Philip Larkin, John Wain, Elizabeth Jennings and Thom Gunn. In the 1990s, interest in 'The Movement' resurfaced with the rise of New Formalism, when the more formal qualities of poetry began to be considered important; Philip Larkin's tight control of form was much admired.

Another group of poets whose work came into significance in the 1960s was known as the Liverpool Poets. Their poetry was suitable for live performance and was characterized by more simple language and, frequently, humour. Adrian Henri, Roger McGough and Brian Patten were the most famous of the Liverpool Poets, and led the way for other performance-based poets such as Benjamin Zephaniah. McGough, along with Mike McCartney (brother of the Beatle Paul McCartney) and John Gorman also formed the musical group The Scaffold in 1963, which lasted until 1974. Adrian Henri was a member for a time.

Such work has done much to capture the imagination of young people, and poetry-reading festivals, music concerts and competitions have promoted the genre and added to its popularity. Internationally, the work of singer-songwriters such as Bob Dylan has done much to blur the line between pop musician and poet.

The way has also been paved for more local and regional voices, in particular Ian McMillan from Barnsley and Simon Armitage from Huddersfield, both of whom frequently feature on radio and television. Poets writing in English have increasingly focused on their individual identity and the questions it raises – for example Seamus Heaney in Northern Ireland, R.S. Thomas and Owen Sheers in Wales, Charles Causley in Cornwall and Liz Lochhead in Scotland.

In the latter part of the twentieth century and the beginning of the twenty-first, a new generation of poets has emerged. Alongside Simon Armitage and Owen Sheers (mentioned above), Carol Ann Duffy, Gillian Clarke and Wendy Cope have shown the ability to connect with the people and capture the popular imagination.

Owen Sheers is one of the new generation of poets who have created a fresh readership for their work

New voices, new techniques

There has been a growth in the number of women novelists and short story writers, many of whom have been concerned to highlight women's struggle for identity in a society, indeed in a world, which continues to be male-dominated. Margaret Atwood, Alice Munro and Rose Tremain have well-established reputations, as have Doris Lessing, Anita Desai, Michèle Roberts, A.S. Byatt and Jill Paton Walsh. More recent women writers include Kiran Desai, Kate Grenville, Charlotte Mendelson, and Zadie Smith.

For many authors the interest has been in the writing process and the role of the writer. For example, John Fowles in *The French Lieutenant's Woman* (see page 43) advances the idea of the author in the role of God, while paradoxically suggesting that his characters determine their own life events. Fowles briefly becomes a character in his own text, and plays literary jokes on the reader. The fact that this text has more than one ending links it with the work of Italian Nobel Prize winner Dario Fo, whose 1970 play *Accidental Death of an Anarchist* leaves the audience to decide on the ending. This idea of leaving texts 'unfinished' perhaps reflects the uncertainty of the times in which we live, and a lack of security for some about their own or others' identity.

Increasingly, texts have become **self-reflexive** (where they as it were examine themselves) and there is a post-modern tendency to fragment a text's narrative, as in *Captain Corelli's Mandolin*, or to toy with the reader as does Fowles in *The French Lieutenant's Woman*. There has in addition been a growth of **intertextuality**, where reference is made within a text to the work of another writer. Margaret Atwood, for example, has *Gertrude Talks Back*, in which Hamlet's mother voices her version of the situation at Elsinore, while Angela Carter reworks fairy tales and myths in *The Bloody Chamber* (see page 56) and Benjamin Zephaniah echoes Philip Larkin's *This Be The Verse* (see page 54) with his poem *This Be The Worst* in the collection *Too Black, Too Strong*. Atwood's *The Handmaid's Tale* has an epilogue which (fictionally) reevaluates the narrator Offred's text; Ian McEwan at the end of *Enduring Love* (1977) presents a medical study of de Clerambault's syndrome from which one of the protagonists has allegedly been suffering. The fact that the syndrome exists mainly in the imagination of the writer makes it another example of a literary joke.

More recently Jasper Fforde's *The Eyre Affair* (2001) is set in a parallel world where it is 1984, there is an independent Welsh republic, people keep pet dodos and the Crimean War is still raging. It has a plot strand involving the attempted kidnap of Jane Eyre from Charlotte Brontë's novel of the same name. Fforde has made such intertextuality, which strikes at the core of the integrity of the text, almost his trade mark. More recently Lloyd Jones's *Mr Pip* (see page 83) uses parts of the text of Charles Dickens's *Great Expectations*, and Dickens's character Pip becomes merged for a time with the identity and past life of Mr Watts, self-appointed teacher on a tropical island on which he is the only white man.

The years spanning the latter part of the twentieth century and the beginning of the twenty-first have seen English literature of all genres enriched by the work of writers from a background of other cultures and traditions, such as Maya Angelou, Grace Nichols, Alice Walker, Moniza Alvi, Linton Kwesi Johnson, Wole Soyinka, Ken Saro-Wiwa and Wislawa Szymborska. Their work has sought to explore the role of those marginalized by the society in which they live because of their culture, gender, language, race or class.

South American writers such as Laura Esquivel, Isabel Allende and Gabriel García Márquez, whose works can be read in translation, have embraced **magic realism**, in which the fantastical and that which seems grounded in reality are mixed.

It is also interesting to see how a nation is perceived by outsiders, so Bill Bryson's work is significant in this respect, especially *Notes from a Small Island*, which traces a journey around the UK. *Watching the English* by Kate Fox gives some fascinating insights into what it is to be English, while *Mr Pip* by

New Zealander Lloyd Jones looks at what it is to be white from the point of view of the black population of an island in the southern hemisphere.

A 2007 survey, the results of which were published in *The Times*, singled out some 25 future 'literary lions', including Nigerian-born Helen Oyeyemi, whose novel *The Icarus Girl* was written while still at school; Guatam Malkani, whose *Londonstani* is written in 'rudeboy' patois; Naomi Alderman, whose first novel *Disobedience* is set in the Orthodox Jewish community of North London; and Marina Lewycka, of Ukrainian origin, who was in a German refugee camp, now lives in Sheffield, and whose novel *A Short History of Tractors in Ukrainian* has been translated into over 30 languages. From the above short list it is clear that a focus on a mix of race and culture is the stuff of modern, especially twenty-first-century, literature.

This is an exciting time in which to live due to the energy, imagination and vision of so many new writers, as well as developments in the writings of now well-established ones. What is noticeable is the sheer diversity of voices and approaches, so that each must be looked at on its own terms. What they have in common is their interest in the examination of, and struggle to assert, the individual's identity in a world which constantly holds this up to question and where boundaries are creatively blurred.

The Struggle for Identity
in Modern Literature

A *Doll's House*: Henrik Ibsen

NORA We have been married now eight years. Does it not
occur to you that this is the first time we two, you and
I, husband and wife, have had a serious conversation?

HELMER What do you mean, serious?

NORA In all these eight years – longer than that – from   5
the very beginning of our acquaintance we have
never exchanged a word on any serious subject.

HELMER Was it likely that I would be continually and
forever telling you about worries that you could
not help me to bear?   10

NORA I am not speaking about business matters. I say
that we have never sat down in earnest together to try
and get at the bottom of anything.

HELMER But, dearest Nora, would it have been any good
to you?   15

NORA That is just it; you have never understood me. I
have been greatly wronged, Torvald – first by Papa
and then by you.

HELMER What! By us two – by us two who have loved
you better than anyone else in the world?   20

NORA (*shaking her head*) You have never loved me.
You have only thought it pleasant to be in love with
me.

HELMER Nora, what do I hear you saying?

NORA It is perfectly true, Torvald. When I was at home   25
with Papa he told me his opinion about everything,
and so I had the same opinions; and if I differed from
him I concealed the fact, because he would not have
liked it. He called me his doll child, and he played
with me just as I used to play with my dolls. And   30
when I came to live with you –

HELMER What sort of an expression is that to use about our marriage?

NORA (*undisturbed*) I mean that I was simply transferred from Papa's hands to yours. You arranged everything   35
according to your own taste, and so I got the same tastes as you – or else I pretended to. I am really not quite sure which – I think sometimes the one and sometimes the other. When I look back on it it seems to me as if I have been living here like a poor woman –   40
just from hand to mouth. I have existed merely to perform tricks for you, Torvald. But you would have it so. You and Papa have committed a great sin against me. It is your fault that I have made nothing of my life.   45

HELMER How unreasonable and how ungrateful you are, Nora! Have you not been happy here?

NORA No, I have never been happy. I thought I was, but it has never really been so.

HELMER Not – not happy!   50

NORA No, only merry. And you have always been so kind to me. But our home has been nothing but a play-room. I have been your doll wife, just as at home I was Papa's doll child; and here the children have been my dolls. I thought it great fun when you played with   55
me, just as they thought it great fun when I played with them. That is what our marriage has been, Torvald.

HELMER There is some truth in what you say – exaggerated and strained as your view of it is. But for the future it shall be different. Playtime shall be over   60
and lesson time shall begin.

NORA Whose lessons? Mine or the children's?

HELMER Both yours and the children's, my darling Nora.

NORA Alas, Torvald, you are not the man to educate me into being a proper wife for you.   65

HELMER And you can say that!

NORA And I – how am I fitted to bring up the children?

HELMER Nora!

NORA Didn't you say so yourself a little while ago – that you dare not trust me to bring them up?   70

HELMER In a moment of anger! Why do you pay any heed to that?

NORA Indeed, you were perfectly right. I am not fit for the task. There is another task I must undertake first. I must try and educate myself – you are not the man   75 to help me in that. I must do that for myself. And that is why I am going to leave you now.

HELMER (*springing up*) What do you say?

NORA I must stand quite alone if I am to understand myself and everything about me. It is for that reason   80 that I cannot remain with you any longer.

HELMER Nora, Nora!

NORA I am going away from here now, at once.

The House of Bernarda Alba: Federico García Lorca

ADELA (*close before her*) He loves me, *me*! He loves me, *me*!

MARTIRIO Stick me with a knife if you like, but don't tell me that again.

ADELA That's why you're trying to fix it so I won't   5 go away with him. It makes no difference to you if he puts his arms around a woman he doesn't love. Nor does it to me. He could be a hundred years with Angustias, but for him to have his arms around me

seems terrible to you – because you too love him! You 10
love him!

MARTIRIO (*dramatically*) Yes! Let me say it without hiding
my head. Yes! My breast's bitter, bursting like a pomegranate. I love him!

ADELA (*impulsively, hugging her*) Martirio, Martirio, I'm 15
not to blame!

MARTIRIO Don't put your arms around me! Don't try
to smooth it over. My blood's no longer yours, and
even though I try to think of you as a sister, I see you
as just another woman. 20

> *She pushes her away.*

ADELA There's no way out here. Whoever has to drown –
let her drown. Pepe is mine. He'll carry me to the
rushes along the riverbank...

MARTIRIO He won't!

ADELA I can't stand this horrible house after the taste 25
of his mouth. I'll be what he wants me to be.
Everybody in the village against me, burning me with
their fiery fingers; pursued by those who claim
they're decent, and I'll wear, before them all, the
crown of thorns that belongs to the mistress of a 30
married man.

MARTIRIO Hush!

ADELA Yes, yes.

> *In a low voice*

Let's go to bed. Let's let him marry Angustias. I don't
care any more, but I'll go off alone to a little house 35
where he'll come to see me whenever he wants, whenever he feels like it.

MARTIRIO That'll never happen! Not while I have a drop
of blood left in my body.

ADELA Not just weak you, but a wild horse I could force 40
to his knees with just the strength of my little finger.

MARTIRIO Don't raise that voice of yours to me. It irritates me. I have a heart full of a force so evil that, without my wanting to be, I'm drowned by it.

ADELA You show us the way to love our sisters. God must   45
have meant to leave me alone in the midst of darkness, because I can see you as I've never seen you before.

> *A whistle is heard and Adela runs toward the door, but Martirio gets in front of her.*

MARTIRIO Where are you going?

ADELA Get away from that door!

MARTIRIO Get by me if you can!   50

ADELA Get away!

> *They struggle.*

MARTIRIO (*shouts*) Mother! Mother!

ADELA Let me go!

> *Bernarda enters. She wears petticoats and a black shawl.*

BERNARDA Quiet! Quiet! How poor I am without even
a man to help me!   55

MARTIRIO (*pointing to Adela*) She was with him. Look at those skirts covered with straw!

BERNARDA (*going furiously toward Adela*) That's the bed of a bad woman!

ADELA (*facing her*) There'll be an end to prison voices   60
here!

> *Adela snatches away her mother's cane and breaks it in two.*

This is what I do with the tyrant's cane. Not another step. No one but Pepe commands me!

> *Magdalena enters.*

MAGDALENA Adela!

> *Poncia and Angustias enter.*

ADELA I'm his.   65

> *To Angustias*

Know that – and go out in the yard and tell him. He'll be master in this house.

ANGUSTIAS My God!

BERNARDA The gun! Where's the gun?

> *She rushes out. Poncia runs ahead of her. Amelia enters and looks on frightened, leaning her head against the wall. Behind her comes Martirio.*

ADELA No one can hold me back! 70

> *She tries to go out.*

ANGUSTIAS (*holding her*) You're not getting out of here with your body's triumph! Thief! Disgrace of this house!

MAGDALENA Let her go where we'll never see her again!

> *A shot is heard.*

BERNARDA (*entering*) Just try looking for him now! 75

MARTIRIO (*entering*) That does away with Pepe el Romano.

ADELA Pepe! My God! Pepe!

> *She runs out.*

PONCIA Did you kill him?

MARTIRIO No. He raced away on his mare! 80

BERNARDA It was my fault. A woman can't aim.

MAGDALENA Then, why did you say... ?

MARTIRIO For her! I'd like to pour a river of blood over her head!

PONCIA Curse you! 85

MAGDALENA Devil!

BERNARDA Although it's better this way!

> *A thud is heard.*

Adela! Adela!

PONCIA (*at her door*) Open this door!

BERNARDA Open! Don't think the walls will hide your 90 shame!

SERVANT (*entering*) All the neighbours are up!

BERNARDA (*in a low voice, but like a roar*) Open! Or
I'll knock the door down!
> *Pause. Everything is silent.*

Adela!   95
> *She walks away from the door.*

A hammer!
> *Poncia throws herself against the door. It opens and*
> *she goes in. As she enters, she screams and backs out.*

What is it?
PONCIA (*she puts her hands to her throat*) May we never
die like that!
> *The sisters fall back. The servant crosses herself.*
> *Bernarda screams and goes forward.*

Don't go in!   100
BERNARDA No, not I! Pepe, you're running now, alive,
in the darkness, under the trees, but another day you'll
fall. Cut her down! My daughter died a virgin. Take
her to another room and dress her as though she were
a virgin. No one will say anything about this! She died 105
a virgin. Tell them, so that at dawn, the bells will ring
twice.
MARTIRIO A thousand times happy she who had him.
BERNARDA And I want no weeping. Death must be
looked at face to face. Silence!   110
> *To one daughter*

Be still, I said!
> *To another daughter*

Tears when you're alone! We'll drown ourselves in a
sea of mourning. She, the youngest daughter of
Bernarda Alba, died a virgin. Did you hear me?
Silence, silence, I said. Silence!   115

The Glass Menagerie: Tennessee Williams

TOM What in Christ's name am I –
AMANDA (*shrilly*) Don't you use that –
TOM Supposed to do!
AMANDA Expression! Not in my –
TOM Ohhh!   5
AMANDA Presence! Have you gone out of your senses?
TOM I have, that's true, *driven* out!
AMANDA What is the matter with you, you – big – big
  IDIOT!
TOM Look! – I've got *no thing,* no single thing –   10
AMANDA Lower your voice!
TOM In my life here that I can call my OWN! Everything
  is –
AMANDA Stop that shouting!
TOM Yesterday you confiscated my books! You had   15
  the nerve to –
AMANDA I took that horrible novel back to the library –
  yes! That hideous book by that insane Mr Lawrence.
  (*Tom laughs wildly.*) I cannot control the output of
  diseased minds or people who cater to them – (*Tom*   20
  laughs still more wildly.) BUT I WON'T ALLOW SUCH FILTH
  BROUGHT INTO MY HOUSE! No no, no, no, no!
TOM House, house! Who pays rent on it, who makes a
  slave of himself to –
AMANDA (*fairly screeching*) Don't you DARE to –   25
TOM No, no, I mustn't say things! *I've* got to just –
AMANDA Let me tell you –
TOM I don't want to hear any more! (*He tears the portières*
  open. The upstage area is lit with a turgid smoky red glow.)

Amanda's hair is in metal curlers and she wears a very old bathrobe, much too large for her slight figure, a relic of the faithless Mr Wingfield. An upright typewriter and a wild disarray of manuscripts are on the drop-leaf table. The quarrel was probably precipitated by Amanda's interruption of his creative labour. A chair lying overthrown on the floor.

Their gesticulating shadows are cast on the ceiling by the fiery glow.

AMANDA You *will* hear more, you –

TOM No, I won't hear more, I'm going out!   30

All My Sons: Arthur Miller

CHRIS I kissed you...

ANN Like Larry's brother. Do it like you, Chris. (*He breaks away from her abruptly.*) What is it, Chris?

CHRIS Let's drive some place... I want to be alone with you.   5

ANN No... what is it, Chris, your mother?

CHRIS No – nothing like that.

ANN Then what's wrong? Even in your letters, there was something ashamed.

CHRIS Yes. I suppose I have been. But it's going from me.   10

ANN You've got to tell me –

CHRIS I don't know how to start. (*He takes her hand.*)

ANN It wouldn't work this way. (*Slight pause.*)

CHRIS (*speaks quietly, factually at first*) It's all mixed up with so many other things... You remember overseas, I was in command of a company?   15

ANN Yeah, sure.

CHRIS Well, I lost them.

ANN How many? 20

CHRIS Just about all.

ANN Oh, gee!

CHRIS It takes a little time to toss that off. Because they weren't just men. For instance, one time it'd been raining several days and this kid came to me, and 25 gave me his last pair of dry socks. Put them in my pocket. That's only a little thing – but... that's the kind of guys I had. They didn't die; they killed themselves for each other. I mean that exactly; a little more selfish and they'd 've been here today. And I 30 got an idea – watching them go down. Everything was being destroyed, see, but it seemed to me that one new thing was made. A kind of – responsibility. Man for man. You understand me? – To show that, to bring that on to the earth again like some kind of 35 a monument and everyone would feel it standing there, behind him, and it would make a difference to him. (*Pause.*) And then I came home and it was incredible. I – there was no meaning in it here; the whole thing to them was a kind of a – bus accident. 40 I went to work with Dad, and that rat-race again. I felt – what you said – ashamed somehow. Because nobody was changed at all. It seemed to make suckers out of a lot of guys. I felt wrong to be alive, to open the bank-book, to drive the new car, to see the new 45 refrigerator. I mean you can take those things out of a war, but when you drive that car you've got to know that it came out of the love a man can have for a man, you've got to be a little better because of that. Otherwise what you have is really loot, and there's 50 blood on it. I didn't want to take any of it. And I guess that included you.

The Go-Between: L.P. Hartley

Now that I was thirteen I was under an obligation to look reality in the face. At school I should be one of the older boys to whom the others looked up. When I thought of last night's performance at the outhouse, of my efforts to impose my puny self upon events, when I thought of my career as a magician, the mumbo-jumbo which I had practised and which I had taught to others, I grew hot. And my letter to my mother – that pitiful petition for recall – how I despised myself for writing it. Looking back on my actions since I came to Brandham, I condemned them all: they seemed the actions of another person.

I condemned them unheard. I did not stop to ask myself how, if they were to do again, I should improve on them. I saw them all as instances of a gross piece of quackery, that had begun the moment I arrived at Brandham – had indeed begun before, when Jenkins and Strode had fallen off the roof. Ever since then I had been playing a part, which seemed to have taken in everybody, and most of all myself. It would not have taken in my old nurse, who had been very quick to spot in me, or any child, a tendency to ape an alien personality. She had no objection to one's being any kind of animal, or any kind of human being, high or low, young or old, dead or alive, provided it was a pretence, provided you could say *who* you were, when challenged. But if the assumed personality was a distortion of one's own ego, the 'I' decked out in borrowed plumes meant to impress, somebody one would like to be thought to be, then she was down on one. 'Who are you being now?' she would ask me. 'Oh, nobody special. Just Leo.'

27

'Well, you're not my Leo. You're another little boy and I don't like him.'

All the time at Brandham I had been another little boy and the grown-ups had aided and abetted me in this: it was a great deal their fault. They like to think of a little boy as a little boy, corresponding to their idea of what a little boy should be – as a representative of little boyhood – not a Leo or a Marcus. They even had a special language designed for little boys – at least some of them had, some of the visitors: not the family: the family, and Lord Trimingham too who was soon to be one of them, respected one's dignity. But there are other ways, far more seductive to oneself than the title 'my little man', to make one feel unreal. No little boy likes to be called a little man, but any little boy likes to be treated as a little man, and this is what Marian had done for me: at times, and when she had wanted to, she had endowed me with the importance of a grown-up; she had made me feel that she depended on me. She, more than anyone, had puffed me up.

The Thought-Fox: Ted Hughes

I imagine this midnight moment's forest:
Something else is alive
Beside the clock's loneliness
And this blank page where my fingers move.

Through the window I see no star:
Something more near
Though deeper within darkness
Is entering the loneliness:

Cold, delicately as the dark snow
A fox's nose touches twig, leaf;   10
Two eyes serve a movement, that now
And again now, and now, and now

Sets neat prints into the snow
Between trees, and warily a lame
Shadow lags by stump and in hollow   15
Of a body that is bold to come

Across clearings, an eye,
A widening deepening greenness,
Brilliantly, concentratedly,
Coming about its own business   20

Till, with a sudden sharp hot stink of fox
It enters the dark hole of the head.
The window is starless still; the clock ticks,
The page is printed.

Things Fall Apart: Chinua Achebe

Okonkwo ruled his household with a heavy hand. His
wives, especially the youngest, lived in perpetual fear of
his fiery temper, and so did his little children. Perhaps
down in his heart Okonkwo was not a cruel man. But
his whole life was dominated by fear, the fear of failure   5
and of weakness. It was deeper and more intimate than
the fear of evil and capricious gods and of magic, the
fear of the forest, and the forces of nature, malevolent,
red in tooth and claw. Okonkwo's fear was greater than
these. It was not external but lay deep within himself.   10

It was the fear of himself, lest he should be found to resemble his father. Even as a little boy he had resented his father's failure and weakness, and even now he still remembered how he had suffered when a playmate had told him that his father was *agbala*. That was how Okonkwo first came to know that *agbala* was not only another name for a woman, it could also mean a man who had taken no title. And so Okonkwo was ruled by one passion – to hate everything that his father Unoka had loved. One of those things was gentleness and another was idleness.

During the planting season Okonkwo worked daily on his farms from cock-crow until the chickens went to roost. He was a very strong man and rarely felt fatigue. But his wives and young children were not as strong, and so they suffered. But they dared not complain openly. Okonkwo's first son, Nwoye, was then twelve years old but was already causing his father great anxiety for his incipient laziness. At any rate, that was how it looked to his father, and he sought to correct him by constant nagging and beating. And so Nwoye was developing into a sad-faced youth.

For three years Ikemefuna lived in Okonkwo's household and the elders of Umuofia seemed to have forgotten about him. He grew rapidly like a yam tendril in the rainy season, and was full of the sap of life. He had become wholly absorbed into his new family. He was like an elder brother to Nwoye, and from the very first seemed to have kindled a new fire in the younger boy. He made him feel grown-up; and they no longer spent the evenings in mother's hut while she cooked, but now sat with Okonkwo in his *obi*, or watched him as he tapped his palm tree for the evening wine. Nothing

pleased Nwoye now more than to be sent for by his
mother or another of his father's wives to do one of   45
those difficult and masculine tasks in the home, like
splitting wood, or pounding food. On receiving such a
message through a younger brother or sister, Nwoye
would feign annoyance and grumble aloud about women
and their troubles.   50

Okonkwo was inwardly pleased at his son's development, and he knew it was due to Ikemefuna. He wanted
Nwoye to grow into a tough young man capable of ruling
his father's household when he was dead and gone to
join the ancestors. He wanted him to be a prosperous   55
man, having enough in his barn to feed the ancestors
with regular sacrifices. And so he was always happy when
he heard him grumbling about women. That showed
that in time he would be able to control his women-
folk. No matter how prosperous a man was, if he was   60
unable to rule his women and his children (and especially his women) he was not really a man. He was like
the man in the song who had ten and one wives and not
enough soup for his foo-foo.

So Okonkwo encouraged the boys to sit with him in   65
his *obi*, and he told them stories of the land – masculine stories of violence and bloodshed. Nwoye knew
that it was right to be masculine and to be violent, but
somehow he still preferred the stories that his mother
used to tell, and which she no doubt still told to her   70
younger children – stories of the tortoise and his wily
ways, and of the bird *eneke-nti-oba* who challenged the
whole world to a wrestling contest and was finally
thrown by the cat. He remembered the story she often
told of the quarrel between Earth and Sky long ago, and 75
how Sky withheld rain for seven years, until crops with-
ered and the dead could not be buried because the hoes

broke on the stony Earth. At last Vulture was sent to plead with Sky, and to soften his heart with a song of the suffering of the sons of men. Whenever Nwoye's 80 mother sang this song he felt carried away to the distant scene in the sky where Vulture, Earth's emissary, sang for mercy. At last Sky was moved to pity, and he gave to Vulture rain wrapped in leaves of coco-yam. But as he flew home his long talon pierced the leaves and the 85 rain fell as it had never fallen before. And so heavily did it rain on Vulture that he did not return to deliver his message but flew to a distant land, from where he had espied a fire. And when he got there he found it was a man making a sacrifice. He warmed himself in the fire 90 and ate the entrails.

That was the kind of story that Nwoye loved. But he now knew that they were for foolish women and children, and he knew that his father wanted him to be a man. And so he feigned that he no longer cared for women's 95 stories. And when he did this he saw that his father was pleased, and no longer rebuked him or beat him.

The Prisoner: Amiya Rao

– the marriage is solemnised.
At an auspicious hour of a starlit night
the father gives the daughter away to a man he does not
    know quite
knotted to a stranger – the husband to be – just behind
    him seven
seven times round the fire, modestly careful, seven small
    steps takes she 5

bowing her veiled head, she accepts her destiny and
    becomes his wife
    and enters new life.

In the father-in-law's house under the eye of the mother-
    in-law queen,
in the maddening jungle of inquisitive in-laws – sisters,
    brothers, cousins, easily umpteen –
days pass, become months, then years – round the clock   10
cook food, serve guests, wash plates, tend the old, nurse
    the sick
on the move from the kitchen to the bedroom to the
    lean-to
the flood is on, sons come, follow daughters –
some die, some remain
a little joy, more pain –   15
two slave chained together, whipped by life
no time to sit together, chat together, laugh together,
    know each other
– no time to shed tears –
Why does the spring come, the cuckoo call and the trees
    sing
– Who hears?   20

'You fool, the cuckoo calls for you to hear', says the
    sari
'the trees sing for you to laugh, not to fear' says the sari
'the spring has come to fill your heart' says the sari
'You fool, I am here for you to wear' says the sari
'have me on', pleads the sari   25
'my angry purple grown soft with age will hide your
    pallor well,
my border, now like the sun when the day is dying, will
    hide those streaks of grey

33

my russet petals yellow tinged with approach of winter
　will sigh for that lissom body
– but sighing will embrace you – with grace
take me out, wear me once, time is passing,' sobs the sari.　　30

Sighing the busy housewife says 'I know what you say
　is true
yet I must rush, have to go, get ready, have a lot to do
My mother-in-law's great Guru will be here in an hour
　or two
and with him will come his disciples, at least fifty-two.
So – not now, not now, some other time, later maybe,
　you see　　35
I must fly, time is passing'.
'I can see' sobs the sari 'time is passing'.

Days have passed become months become years
Alone in the darkening shadows sits she musing
– life is nothing only tears –　　40
'You are right,' whispers the sari, all in tatters
– 'Life is nothing only tears.'

Song of Lawino: Okot p'Bitek

The Woman With Whom I Share My Husband

Ocol rejects the old type.
He is in love with a modern woman,
He is in love with a beautiful girl
Who speaks English.

But only recently　　5
We would sit close together, touching each other!

Only recently I would play
On my bow-harp
Singing praises to my beloved.
Only recently he promised   10
That he trusted me completely.
I used to admire him speaking in English.

Ocol is no longer in love with the old type;
He is in love with a modern girl.
The name of the beautiful one   15
Is Clementine.

Brother, when you see Clementine!
The beautiful one aspires
To look like a white woman;

Her lips are red-hot   20
Like glowing charcoal,
She resembles the wild cat
That has dipped its mouth in blood,
Her mouth is like raw yaws
It looks like an open ulcer,   25
Like the mouth of a field!
Tina dusts powder on her face
And it looks so pale;
She resembles the wizard
Getting ready for the midnight dance.   30

She dusts the ash-dirt all over her face
And when little sweat
Begins to appear on her body
She looks like the guinea fowl!

The smell of carbolic soap   35
Makes me sick,

And the smell of powder
Provokes the ghosts in my head;
It is then necessary to fetch a goat
From my mother's brother.   40
The sacrifice over
The ghost-dance drum must sound
The ghost be laid
And my peace restored.

I do not like dusting myself with powder: 45
The thing is good on pink skin
Because it is already pale,
But when a black woman has used it
She looks as if she has dysentery;
Tina looks sickly   50
And she is slow moving,
She is a piteous sight.

Some medicine has eaten up Tina's face;
The skin on her face is gone
And it is all raw and red,   55
The face of the beautiful one
Is tender like the skin of a newly born baby!

And she believes
That this is beautiful
Because it resembles the face of a white woman!   60
Her body resembles
The ugly coat of the hyena;
Her neck and arms
Have real human skins!
She looks as if she has been struck   65
By lightning;

Or burnt like the kongoni
In a fire hunt.
And her lips look like bleeding,
Her hair is long   70
Her head is huge like that of the owl,
She looks like a witch,
Like someone who has lost her head
And should be taken
To the clan shrine!   75
Her neck is rope-like,
Thin, long and skinny
And her face sickly pale.

Forgive me, brother,
Do not think I am insulting   80
The woman with whom I share my husband!
Do not think my tongue
Is being sharpened by jealousy.
It is the sight of Tina
That provokes sympathy from my heart.   85

I do not deny
I am a little jealous.
It is no good lying,
We all suffer from a little jealousy.
It catches you unawares   90
Like the ghosts that bring fevers;
It surprises people
Like earth tremors:
But when you see the beautiful woman
With whom I share my husband   95
You feel a little pity for her!

Her breasts are completely shrivelled up,
They are all folded dry skins,
They have made nests of cotton wool
And she folds the bits of cow-hide   100
In the nests
And call them breasts!

O! my clansmen
How aged modern women
Pretend to be young girls!   105

They mould the tips of the cotton nests
So that they are sharp
And with these they prick
The chests of their men!
And the men believe   110
They are holding the waists
Of young girls that have just shot up!
The modern type sleep with their nests
Tied firmly on their chests.
How many kids   115
Has this woman sucked?
The empty bags on her chest
Are completely flattened, dried.

Digging: Seamus Heaney

Between my finger and my thumb
The squat pen rests; snug as a gun.

Under my window, a clean rasping sound
When the spade sinks into gravelly ground:
My father, digging. I look down   5

Till his straining rump among the flowerbeds
Bends low, comes up twenty years away
Stooping in rhythm through potato drills
Where he was digging.

The coarse boot nestled on the lug, the shaft   10
Against the inside knee was levered firmly.
He rooted out tall tops, buried the bright edge deep
To scatter new potatoes that we picked
Loving their cool hardness in our hands.

By God, the old man could handle a spade.   15
Just like his old man.

My grandfather cut more turf in a day
Than any other man on Toner's bog.
Once I carried him milk in a bottle
Corked sloppily with paper. He straightened up   20
To drink it, then fell to right away

Nicking and slicing neatly, heaving sods
Over his shoulder, going down and down
For the good turf. Digging.

The cold smell of potato mould, the squelch and slap   25
Of soggy peat, the curt cuts of an edge
Through living roots awaken in my head.
But I've no spade to follow men like them.

Between my finger and my thumb
The squat pen rests.   30
I'll dig with it.

Follower: Seamus Heaney

My father worked with a horse-plough,
His shoulders globed like a full sail strung
Between the shafts and the furrow.
The horses strained at his clicking tongue.

An expert. He would set the wing   5
And fit the bright steel-pointed sock.
The sod rolled over without breaking.
At the headrig, with a single pluck

Of reins, the sweating team turned round
And back into the land. His eye   10
Narrowed and angled at the ground,
Mapping the furrow exactly.

I stumbled in his hob-nailed wake,
Fell sometimes on the polished sod;
Sometimes he rode me on his back   15
Dipping and rising to his plod.

I wanted to grow up and plough,
To close one eye, stiffen my arm.
All I ever did was follow
In his broad shadow round the farm.   20

I was a nuisance, tripping, falling,
Yapping always. But today
It is my father who keeps stumbling
Behind me, and will not go away.

The Early Purges: Seamus Heaney

I was six when I first saw kittens drown,
Dan Taggart pitched them, 'the scraggy wee shits',
Into a bucket; a frail metal sound,

Soft paws scraping like mad. But their tiny din
Was soon soused. They were slung on the snout   5
Of the pump and the water pumped in.

'Sure isn't it better for them now?' Dan said.
Like wet gloves they bobbed and shone till he sluiced
Them out on the dunghill, glossy and dead.

Suddenly frightened, for days I sadly hung   10
Round the yard, watching the three sogged remains
Turn mealy and crisp as old summer dung

Until I forgot them. But the fear came back
When Dan trapped big rats, snared rabbits, shot crows
Or, with a sickening tug, pulled old hens' necks.   15

Still, living displaces false sentiments
And now, when shrill pups are prodded to drown
I just shrug, 'Bloody pups'. It makes sense:

'Prevention of cruelty' talk cuts ice in town.
Where they consider death unnatural,   20
But on well-run farms pests have to be kept down.

The Joy of Writing: Wislawa Szymborska

Why does this written doe bound through these written
    woods?
For a drink of written water from a spring
whose surface will xerox her soft muzzle?
Why does she lift her head; does she hear something?
Perched on four slim legs borrowed from the truth,   5
she pricks up her ears beneath my fingertips.
Silence – this word also rustles across the page
and parts the boughs
that have sprouted from the word 'woods.'

Lying in wait, set to pounce on the blank page,   10
are letters up to no good,
clutches of clauses so subordinate
they'll never let her get away.

Each drop of ink contains a fair supply
of hunters, equipped with squinting eyes behind their
    sights,   15
prepared to swarm the sloping pen at any moment,
surround the doe, and slowly aim their guns.

They forget that what's here isn't life.
Other laws, black on white, obtain.
The twinkling of an eye will take as long as I say,   20
and will, if I wish, divide into tiny eternities,
full of bullets stopped in mid-flight.

Not a thing will ever happen unless I say so.
Without my blessing, not a leaf will fall,
not a blade of grass will bend beneath that little hoof's
    full stop.   25

Is there then a world
where I rule absolutely on fate?
A time I bind with chains of signs?
An existence become endless at my bidding?

The joy of writing.   30
The power of preserving.
Revenge of a mortal hand.

The French Lieutenant's Woman: John Fowles

I do not know. This story I am telling is all imagination.
These characters I create never existed outside my own
mind. If I have pretended until now to know my characters' minds and innermost thoughts, it is because I am
writing in (just as I have assumed some of the vocabu-   5
lary and 'voice' of) a convention universally accepted at
the time of my story: that the novelist stands next to
God. He may not know all, yet he tries to pretend that
he does. But I live in the age of Alain Robbe-Grillet and
Roland Barthes; if this is a novel, it cannot be a novel   10
in the modern sense of the word.

    So perhaps I am writing a transposed autobiography;
perhaps I now live in one of the houses I have brought

into the fiction; perhaps Charles is myself disguised. Perhaps it is only a game. Modern women like Sarah exist, and I have never understood them. Or perhaps I am trying to pass off a concealed book of essays on you. Instead of chapter headings, perhaps I should have written 'On the Horizontality of Existence', 'The Illusions of Progress', 'The History of the Novel Form', 'The Aetiology of Freedom', 'Some Forgotten Aspects of the Victorian Age'... what you will.

Perhaps you suppose that a novelist has only to pull the right strings and his puppets will behave in a lifelike manner; and produce on request a thorough analysis of their motives and intentions. Certainly I intended at this stage (*Chap. Thirteen – unfolding of Sarah's true state of mind*) to tell all – or all that matters. But I find myself suddenly like a man in the sharp spring night, watching from the lawn beneath that dim upper window in Marlborough House; I know in the context of my book's reality that Sarah would never have brushed away her tears and leant down and delivered a chapter of revelation. She would instantly have turned, had she seen me there just as the old moon rose, and disappeared into the interior shadows.

But I am a novelist, not a man in a garden – I can follow her where I like. But possibility is not permissibility. Husbands could often murder their wives – and the reverse – and get away with it. But they don't.

You may think novelists always have fixed plans to which they work, so that the future predicted by Chapter One is always inexorably the actuality of Chapter Thirteen. But novelists write for countless different reasons: for money, for fame, for reviewers, for parents, for friends, for loved ones; for vanity, for pride, for curiosity, for amusement: as skilled furniture-makers enjoy making furniture, as drunkards like drinking, as judges like judging, as Sicilians like emptying a shotgun into an enemy's back. I could fill a book with reasons, and they would all be true, though not true of all. Only one same reason is shared by all of us: *we wish to create worlds as real as, but other than the world that is.* Or was. This is why we cannot plan. We know a world is an organism, not a machine. We also know that a genuinely created world must be independent of its creator; a planned world (a world that fully reveals its planning) is a dead world. It is only when our characters and events begin to disobey us that they begin to live. When Charles left Sarah on her cliff-edge, I ordered him to walk straight back to Lyme Regis. But he did not; he gratuitously turned and went down to the Dairy.

Oh, but you say, come on – what I really mean is that the idea crossed my mind as I wrote that it might be more clever to have him stop and drink milk... and meet Sarah again. That is certainly one explanation of what happened; but I can only report – and I am the most reliable witness – that the idea seemed to me to come clearly from Charles, not myself. It is not only that he has begun to gain an autonomy; I must respect it, and disrespect all my quasi-divine plans for him, if I wish him to be real.

In other words, to be free myself, I must give him, and Tina, and Sarah, even the abominable Mrs Poulteney, their freedoms as well. There is only one good definition of God: the freedom that allows other freedoms to exist. And I must conform to that definition.

The novelist is still a god, since he creates (and not even the most aleatory avant-garde modern novel has managed to extirpate its author completely); what has changed is that we are no longer the gods of the Victorian image, omniscient and decreeing; but in the new theological image, with freedom our first principle, not authority. 85

I have disgracefully broken the illusion? No. My characters still exist, and in a reality no less, or no more, real than the one I have just broken. Fiction is woven into all, as a Greek observed some two and a half thousand years ago. I find this new reality (or unreality) more 90 valid; and I would have you share my own sense that I do not fully control these creatures of my mind, any more than you control – however hard you try, however much of a latter-day Mrs Poulteney you may be – your 95 children, colleagues, friends or even yourself.

But this is preposterous? A character is either 'real' or 'imaginary'? If you think that, *hypocrite lecteur*, I can only smile. You do not even think of your own past as quite real; you dress it up, you gild it or blacken it, censor 100 it, tinker with it... fictionalize it, in a word, and put it away on a shelf – your book, your romanced autobiography. We are all in flight from the real reality. That is a basic definition of *Homo sapiens*.

So if you think all this unlucky (but it *is* Chapter 105 Thirteen) digression has nothing to do with your Time, Progress, Society, Evolution and all those other capitalized ghosts in the night that are rattling their chains behind the scenes of this book... I will not argue. But I shall suspect you. 110

I Know Why the Caged Bird Sings:
Maya Angelou

In our society, where two-legged, two-armed strong Black men were able at best to eke out only the necessities of life, Uncle Willie, with his starched shirts, shined shoes and shelves full of food, was the whipping boy and butt of jokes of the underemployed and underpaid. Fate not only disabled him but laid a double-tiered barrier in his path. He was also proud and sensitive. Therefore he couldn't pretend that he wasn't crippled, nor could he deceive himself that people were not repelled by his defect.

Only once in all the years of trying not to watch him, I saw him pretend to himself and others that he wasn't lame.

Coming home from school one day, I saw a dark car in our front yard. I rushed in to find a strange man and woman (Uncle Willie said later they were schoolteachers from Little Rock) drinking Dr Pepper in the cool of the Store. I sensed a wrongness around me, like an alarm clock that had gone off without being set.

I knew it couldn't be the strangers. Not frequently, but often enough, travelers pulled off the main road to buy tobacco or soft drinks in the only Negro store in Stamps. When I looked at Uncle Willie, I knew what was pulling my mind's coattails. He was standing erect behind the counter, not leaning forward or resting on the small shelf that had been built for him. Erect. His eyes seemed to hold me with a mixture of threats and appeal.

I dutifully greeted the strangers and roamed my eyes around for his walking stick. It was nowhere to be seen.

He said, 'Uh... this this... this... uh, my niece. She's...
uh... just come from school.' Then to the couple – 'You
know... how, uh, children are... th–th–these days... they
play all d–d–day at school and c–c–can't wait to get home
and pl–play some more.'   35

The people smiled, very friendly.

He added, 'Go on out and pl–play, Sister.'

The lady laughed in a soft Arkansas voice and said,
'Well, you know, Mr Johnson, they say, you're only a
child once. Have you children of your own?'   40

Uncle Willie looked at me with an impatience I hadn't
seen in his face even when he took thirty minutes to
loop the laces over his high-topped shoes. 'I... I thought
I told you to go... go outside and play.'

Before I left I saw him lean back on the shelves of   45
Garret Snuff, Prince Albert and Spark Plug chewing
tobacco.

'No, ma'am... no ch–children and no wife.' He tried
a laugh. 'I have an old m–m–mother and my brother's
t–two children to l–look after.'   50

I didn't mind his using us to make himself look good.
In fact, I would have pretended to be his daughter if he
wanted me to. Not only did I not feel any loyalty to my
own father, I figured that if I had been Uncle Willie's
child I would have received much better treatment.   55

The couple left after a few minutes, and from the back
of the house I watched the red car scare chickens, raise
dust and disappear toward Magnolia.

Uncle Willie was making his way down the long shad-
owed aisle between the shelves and the counter – hand   60
over hand, like a man climbing out of a dream. I stayed
quiet and watched him lurch from one side, bumping
to the other, until he reached the coal-oil tank. He put
his hand behind that dark recess and took his cane in

the strong fist and shifted his weight on the wooden   65
support. He thought he had pulled it off.

I'll never know why it was important to him that the
couple (he said later that he'd never seen them before)
would take a picture of a whole Mr Johnson back to
Little Rock.   70

He must have tired of being crippled, as prisoners tire
of penitentiary bars and the guilty tire of blame. The
high-topped shoes and the cane, his uncontrollable
muscles and thick tongue, and the looks he suffered of
either contempt or pity had simply worn him out, and   75
for one afternoon, one part of an afternoon, he wanted
no part of them.

I understood and felt closer to him at that moment
than ever before or since.

The Female Eunuch: Germaine Greer

Little boys can get out of their mother's way, eventually want to and are encouraged to. Little girls are not.
It is agreed that 'girls take more bringing up' than boys:
what that really means is that girls must be more relentlessly supervised and repressed if the desired result is   5
to ensue. A girl is early introduced to her menial role,
as her mother teaches her household skills (*mirabile
dictu!*) and her recoil from external reality is reinforced
by the punishments she gets for wandering off on her
own. While little boys are forming groups and gangs to   10
explore or terrorize the district, she is isolated at home,
listening to tales of evil-minded strangers. Her comparative incarceration is justified in the name of protection,
although the home is the most dangerous place there is.

She is taught to fear and distrust the world at large, for   15
reasons which are never clearly stated. As a form of fore-
arming this forewarning is notoriously unsuccessful.
Sexual deviates are not so lacking in resource that they
cannot attack little girls as they go upon those errands
and journeys that are sanctioned by Mother. When a   20
little girl who missed her bus rang her mother from the
bus-stop one evening, so spending the sixpence that
would have been her fare for the next one, her mother
told her to walk home because she didn't have the car.
The child went on her way weeping and terrified, and   25
was accosted by a smiling stranger who abducted, raped
and strangled her. The commonest result of the dark
warning system is that when little girls do meet an exhi-
bitionist or do happen to talk to a stranger who does
something odd to them, they are too frightened and   30
guilty, as well as too worried about the effect on their
parents, even to tell them. It is a contributing factor in
the pattern of child violation that little girls think of
themselves as victims, and cannot even summon the
energy to scream or run away. Because they are prevented   35
from understanding the threat, they can have no
adequate defence. The bitterest irony is that the child
violators are themselves products of the same clumsy
conditioning.

While little boys are learning about groups and organ-   40
izations, as well as the nature of the world outside their
homes, little girls are at home, keeping quiet, playing
with dolls and dreaming, or helping Mother. At school
they use their energy to suppress themselves, to be good
and keep quiet, and remember what they are hearing and   45
doing. At home they perform meaningless physical
rituals, with no mental activity attached to them. So the
sensual and intellectual are even more widely separated

in them than they are in their brothers. If the sensual
retains its hold, they prefer to work with their hands,   50
cooking, sewing, knitting, following a pattern designed
by someone else. The designers, the master-cooks and
the tailors are men. If women become 'intellectuals' they
are disenfranchised of their bodies, repressed, intense,
inefficient, still as servile as ever. Some geniuses have   55
broken right through the chain reaction and have seen
it for what it was, but most creative women bear the
stamp of futility and confusion even in their best work.
Virginia Woolf saw some of the way, but it cost her too
much; George Eliot was one of the few who burst right   60
through her straitjacket. The difference may have been
one of the energy of the psyche, or of intelligence, or
simply that Eliot was plain and Virginia was graceful and
lovely. Whatever the case, the foundations of the conflict
were laid in their infancy.   65

The Badness Within Him: Susan Hill

Now, he felt rested, no longer angry, he felt above it
all.

Now, he opened his eyes again and saw his father
striding into the water, until it reached up to his chest:
then he flopped onto his belly and floated for a moment,   5
before beginning to swim.

Col thought, perhaps I am ill and *that* is the badness
within me.

But if he had changed, the others had changed too.
Since Fay had married and had the baby and gone to   10
live in Berkshire, she was different, she fussed more, was
concerned with the details of things, she spoke to them

all a trifle impatiently. And his mother was so languid. And Jess – Jess did not want his company.

Now he saw his father's dark head bobbing up and down quite a long way out to sea, but as he watched, sitting on the high cliff ledge in the sun, the bobbing stopped – began again – an arm came up and waved, though as if it were uncertain of its direction.

Col waved back.

The sun was burning the top of his head.

Fay and Fay's baby and Jess had moved in around the parasol again, their heads were bent together. Col thought, we will never be the same with one another, the ties of blood make no difference, we are separate people now. And then he felt afraid of such truth. Father's waving stopped abruptly, he bobbed and disappeared, bobbed up again.

The sea was still as glass.

Col saw that his father was drowning.

In the end, a man from the other side of the beach went running down to the water's edge and another to where the family were grouped around the parasol. Col looked at the cliff, falling away at his feet. He closed his eyes and turned around slowly and then got down on his hands and knees and began to feel for a foothold, though not daring to look. His head was hot and throbbing.

By the time he reached the bottom, they were bringing his father's body. Col stood in the shadow of the cliff and shivered and smelled the dank, cave smell behind him. His mother and Fay and Jess stood in a line, very erect, like Royalty at the cenotaph, and in Fay's arms the baby was still as a doll.

Everyone else kept away, though Col could see that they made half-gestures, raised an arm or turned a head,

occasionally took an uncertain step forward, before
retreating again.

Eventually he wondered if they had forgotten about
him. The men dripped water off their arms and shoulders as they walked and the sea ran off the body, too,   50
in a thin, steady stream.

Nobody spoke to him about the cliff climb. People
only spoke of baths and hot drinks and telephone
messages, scarcely looking at one another as they did so,
and the house was full of strangers moving from room   55
to room.

In bed, he lay stiffly under the tight sheets and looked
towards the window where the moon shone. He thought,
it is my fault. I prayed for some terrible happening and
the badness within me made it come about. I am   60
punished. For this was a change greater than any he
could have imagined.

They had put his father's body on the trestle, dressed
in a shirt and covered with a sheet and a rug. His head
was bare and lay on a cushion, and the hands, with   65
the black hair over their backs, were folded together.
Now, he was not afraid. His father's skin was oddly pale
and shiny. He stared, trying to feel some sense of loss
and sorrow. He had watched his father drown, though
for a long time he had not believed it, the water had   70
been so entirely calm. Later, he had heard them talking
of a heart attack, and then he had understood better
why this strong barrel of a man, down that day
from the City, should have been so suddenly sinking,
sinking.   75

The fog horn sounded outside. Then, he knew that
the change had come, knew that the long, hot summer
was at an end, and that his childhood had ended too,

that they would never come to this house again. He
knew, finally, the power of the badness within him and   80
because of that, standing close to his father's body, he
wept.

This Be The Verse: Philip Larkin

They fuck you up, your mum and dad.
  They may not mean to, but they do.
They fill you with the faults they had
  And add some extra, just for you.

But they were fucked up in their turn   5
  By fools in old-style hats and coats,
Who half the time were soppy-stern
  And half at one another's throats.

Man hands on misery to man.
  It deepens like a coastal shelf.   10
Get out as early as you can,
  And don't have any kids yourself.

Woman Work: Maya Angelou

I've got the children to tend
The clothes to mend
The floor to mop
The food to shop
Then the chicken to fry   5
The baby to dry

I got company to feed
The garden to weed
I've got the shirts to press
The tots to dress   10
The cane to be cut
I gotta clean up this hut
Then see about the sick
And the cotton to pick.

Shine on me sunshine   15
Rain on me rain
Fall softly, dewdrops
And cool my brow again.

Storm, blow me from here
With your fiercest wind   20
Let me float across the sky
'Til I can rest again.

Fall gently, snowflakes
Cover me with white
Cold icy kisses   25
Let me rest tonight.

Sun, rain, curving sky
Mountain, oceans, leaf and stone
Star shine, moon glow
You're all that I can call my own.   30

The Company of Wolves: Angela Carter

Where is my grandmother?

There's nobody here but we two, my darling.

Now a great howling rose up all around them, near, very near, as close as the kitchen garden, the howling of a multitude of wolves; she knew the worst wolves are hairy on the inside and she shivered, in spite of the scarlet shawl she pulled more closely round herself as if it could protect her although it was as red as the blood she must spill.

Who has come to sing us carols, she said.

Those are the voices of my brothers, darling; I love the company of wolves. Look out of the window and you'll see them.

Snow half-caked the lattice and she opened it to look into the garden. It was a white night of moon and snow; the blizzard whirled round the gaunt, grey beasts who squatted on their haunches among the rows of winter cabbage, pointing their sharp snouts to the moon and howling as if their hearts would break. Ten wolves; twenty wolves – so many wolves she could not count them, howling in concert as if demented or deranged. Their eyes reflected the light from the kitchen and shone like a hundred candles.

It is very cold, poor things, she said; no wonder they howl so.

She closed the window on the wolves' threnody and took off her scarlet shawl, the colour of poppies, the colour of sacrifices, the colour of her menses, and, since her fear did her no good, she ceased to be afraid.

What shall I do with my shawl?

Throw it on the fire, dear one. You won't need it again.

She bundled up her shawl and threw it on the blaze, which instantly consumed it. Then she drew her blouse over her head; her small breasts gleamed as if the snow had invaded the room.   35

What shall I do with my blouse?

Into the fire with it, too, my pet.

The thin muslin went flaring up the chimney like a magic bird and now off came her skirt, her woollen stockings, her shoes, and on to the fire they went, too,   40 and were gone for good. The firelight shone through the edges of her skin; now she was clothed only in her untouched integument of flesh. This dazzling, naked she combed out her hair with her fingers; her hair looked white as the snow outside. Then went directly to the   45 man with red eyes in whose unkempt mane the lice moved; she stood up on tiptoe and unbuttoned the collar of his shirt.

What big arms you have.

All the better to hug you with.   50

Every wolf in the world now howled a prothalamion outside the window as she freely gave the kiss she owed him.

What big teeth you have!

She saw how his jaw began to slaver and the   55 room was full of the clamour of the forest's Liebestod but the wise child never flinched, even when he answered:

All the better to eat you with.

The girl burst out laughing; she knew she was   60 nobody's meat. She laughed at him full in the face, she ripped off his shirt for him and flung it into the fire, in the fiery wake of her own discarded clothing. The flames danced like dead souls on Walpurgisnacht and the old

bones under the bed set up a terrible clattering but she   65
did not pay them any heed.

Carnivore incarnate, only immaculate flesh appeases him.

She will lay his fearful head on her lap and she will
pick out the lice from his pelt and perhaps she will put
the lice into her mouth and eat them, as he will bid her,   70
as she would do in a savage marriage ceremony.

The blizzard will die down.

The blizzard died down, leaving the mountains as
randomly covered with snow as if a blind woman had
thrown a sheet over them, the upper branches of the   75
forest pines limed, creaking, swollen with the fall.

Snowlight, moonlight, a confusion of paw-prints.

All silent, all still.

Midnight; and the clock strikes. It is Christmas Day,
the werewolves' birthday, the door of the solstice stands   80
wide open; let them all sink through.

See! sweet and sound she sleeps in granny's bed,
between the paws of the tender wolf.

Nella Last's War: eds Richard Broad and Suzie Fleming

Thursday, 3 April, 1941

One of our members is in bitter trouble. Her adored
daughter has had a baby and the young soldier father
went East nearly eight months ago and they could not
marry. We have tried to make her happy, and the
daughter went to stay with an aunt in the Lakes. We   5
never mentioned it at all to the mother, beyond a passing
enquiry as to her health. It seems, though, that the poor

girl has fretted badly, both for her own sake – that her
sweetheart could not come home so they could marry –
and for the 'disgrace' she had brought on her mother.   10
The baby, by its snapshot, is such a wistful-eyed, solemn
mite, but there is no hope at all for the mother's recovery.
From apathy and fretting, she has drifted into T.B., and
it's a matter only of a few weeks' more life for her. She
has no interest in her baby, or its father's frantic loving   15
letters that the girl's mother says would 'melt stone' –
such that she cannot bear him hatred for the 'ruin of
her daughter's life' in a way that might seem indicated.
Just another of Hitler's crimes. There was so little we
could say and nothing we could do. Mrs Waite looked   20
so pinched and grey with sympathy and pity.

The Color Purple: Alice Walker

Sofia in jail, I say.
    In jail? She look like I say Sofia on the moon.
    What she in jail for? she ast.
    Sassing the mayor's wife, I say.
    Squeak pull up a chair. Look down my throat.   5
    What your real name? I ast her. She say, Mary Agnes.
    Make Harpo call you by your real name, I say. Then
maybe he see you even when he trouble.
    She look at me puzzle. I let it go. I tell her what one
of Sofia sister tell me and Mr _____.   10
    Sofia and the prizefighter and all the children got in
the prizefighter car and went to town. Clam out on the
street looking like somebody. Just then the mayor and
his wife come by.
    All these children, say the mayor's wife, digging in her   15
pocketbook. Cute as little buttons though, she say. She

stop, put her hand on one of the children head. Say, and such strong white teef.

Sofia and the prizefighter don't say nothing. Wait for her to pass. Mayor wait too, stand back and tap his foot, watch her with a little smile. Now Millie, he say. Always going on over colored. Miss Millie finger the children some more, finally look at Sofia and the prizefighter. She look at the prizefighter car. She eye Sofia wristwatch. She say to Sofia, All your children so clean, she say, would you like to work for me, be my maid?

Sofia say, Hell no.

She say, What you say?

Sofia say, Hell no.

Mayor look at Sofia, push his wife out the way. Stick out his chest. Girl, what you say to Miss Millie?

Sofia say, I say, Hell no.

He slap her.

I stop telling it right there.

Squeak on the edge of her seat. She wait. Look down my throat some more.

No need to say no more, Mr ———— say. You know what happen if somebody slap Sofia.

Squeak go white as a sheet. *Naw*, she say.

Naw nothing, I say. Sofia knock the man down.

When I see Sofia I don't know why she still alive. They crack her skull, they crack her ribs. They tear her nose loose on one side. They blind her in one eye. She swole from head to foot. Her tongue the size of my arm, it stick out tween her teef like a piece of rubber. She can't talk. And she just about the color of a eggplant.

Scare me so bad I near bout drop my grip. But I don't. I put it on the floor of the cell, take out comb and brush, nightgown, witch hazel and alcohol and I start to work on

her. The colored tendant bring me water to wash her with,   50
and I start at her two little slits for eyes.

I Coming Back: Grace Nichols

I coming back Massa
I coming back

mistress of the underworld
I coming back

colour and shape   5
of all that is evil
I coming back

dog howling outside
yuh window
I coming back   10

ball-a-fire
and skinless higue
I coming back

hiss in yuh ear
and prick in yuh skin   15
I coming back

bone in yuh throat
and laugh in yuh skull
I coming back

I coming back Massa   20
I coming back

The Handmaid's Tale: Margaret Atwood

It was after we'd been married, for years it seemed; she was three or four, in daycare.

We'd all got up in the usual way, and had breakfast, granola, I remember, and Luke had driven her off to school, in the little outfit I'd bought her just a couple 5 of weeks before, striped overalls and a blue T-shirt. What month was this? It must have been September. There was a School Pool that was supposed to pick them up, but for some reason I'd wanted Luke to do it, I was getting worried even about the School Pool. No children 10 walked to school any more, there had been too many disappearances.

When I got to the corner store, the usual woman wasn't there. Instead there was a man, a young man, he couldn't have been more than twenty. 15

She sick? I said as I handed him my card.

Who? he said, aggressively I thought.

The woman who's usually here, I said.

How would I know, he said. He was punching my number in, studying each number, punching with one 20 finger. He obviously hadn't done it before. I drummed my fingers on the counter, impatient for a cigarette, wondering if anyone had ever told him something could be done about those pimples on his neck. I remember quite clearly what he looked like: tall, slightly stooped, 25 dark hair cut short, brown eyes that seemed to focus two inches behind the bridge of my nose, and that acne. I suppose I remember him so clearly because of what he said next.

Sorry, he said. This number's not valid. 30

That's ridiculous, I said. It must be, I've got thousands in my account. I just got the statement two days ago. Try it again.

It's not valid, he repeated obstinately. See that red light? Means it's not valid. 35

You must have made a mistake, I said. Try it again.

He shrugged and gave me a fed-up smile, but he did try the number again. This time I watched his fingers, on each number, and checked the numbers that came up in the window. It was my number all right, but there 40 was the red light again.

See? he said again, still with that smile, as if he knew some private joke he wasn't going to tell me.

I'll phone them from the office, I said. The system had fouled up before, but a few phone calls usually 45 straightened it out. Still, I was angry, as if I'd been unjustly accused of something I didn't even know about. As if I'd made the mistake myself.

You do that, he said indifferently. I left the cigarettes on the counter, since I hadn't paid for them. I figured I 50 could borrow some at work.

I did phone from the office, but all I got was a recording. The lines were overloaded, the recording said. Could I please phone back?

The lines stayed overloaded all morning, as far as I 55 could tell. I phoned back several times, but no luck. Even that wasn't too unusual.

About two o'clock, after lunch, the director came in to the discing room.

I have something to tell you, he said. He looked 60 terrible; his hair was untidy, his eyes were pink and wobbling, as though he'd been drinking.

We all looked up, turned off our machines. There must have been eight or ten of us in the room.

I'm sorry, he said, but it's the law. I really am sorry.   65
For what? somebody said.

I have to let you go, he said. It's the law, I have to. I
have to let you all go. He said this almost gently, as if
we were wild animals, frogs he'd caught, in a jar, as if
he were being humane.   70

We're being fired? I said. I stood up. But why?

Not fired, he said. Let go. You can't work here any
more, it's the law. He ran his hands through his hair and
I thought, he's gone crazy. The strain has been too much
for him and he's blown his wiring.   75

You can't just *do* that, said the woman who sat next
to me. This sounded false, improbable, like something
you would say on television.

It isn't me, he said. You don't understand. Please go,
now. His voice was rising. I don't want any trouble. If   80
there's trouble the books might be lost, things will get
broken... He looked over his shoulder. They're outside,
he said, in my office. If you don't go now they'll come
in themselves. They gave me ten minutes. By now he
sounded crazier than ever.   85

He's loopy, someone said out loud; which we must
all have thought.

But I could see out into the corridor, and there were
two men standing there, in uniforms, with machine guns.
This was too theatrical to be true, yet there they were: 90
sudden apparitions, like Martians. There was a dreamlike quality to them; they were too vivid, too at odds
with their surroundings.

Beloved: Toni Morrison

'Mr Garner,' she said, 'why you all call me Jenny?'

''Cause that what's on your sales ticket, gal. Ain't that your name? What you call yourself?'

'Nothing,' she said. 'I don't call myself nothing.'

Mr Garner went red with laughter. 'When I took you   5
out of Carolina, Whitlow called you Jenny and Jenny Whitlow is what his bill said. Didn't he call you Jenny?'

'No, sir. If he did I didn't hear it.'

'What did you answer to?'

'Anything, but Suggs is what my husband name.'   10

'You got married, Jenny? I didn't know it.'

'Manner of speaking.''

'You know where he is, this husband?'

'No, sir.'

'Is that Halle's daddy?'   15

'No, sir.'

'Why you call him Suggs, then? His bill of sale says Whitlow too, just like yours.'

'Suggs is my name, sir. From my husband. He didn't call me Jenny.'   20

'What he call you?'

'Baby.'

'Well,' said Mr Garner going pink again, 'if I was you I'd stick to Jenny Whitlow. Mrs Baby Suggs ain't no name for a freed Negro.'   25

Maybe not, she thought, but Baby Suggs was all she had left of the 'husband' she claimed. A serious, melancholy man who taught her how to make shoes. The two of them made a pact: whichever one got a chance to run would take it; together if possible, alone if not, and no   30
looking back. He got his chance, and since she never

heard otherwise she believed he made it. Now how could he find or hear tell of her if she was calling herself some bill-of-sale name?

She couldn't get over the city. More people than 35 Carolina and enough whitefolks to stop the breath. Two-story buildings everywhere, and walkways made of perfectly cut slats of wood. Roads wide as Garner's whole house.

'This is a city of water,' said Mr Garner. 'Everything 40 travels by water and what the rivers can't carry the canals take. A queen of a city, Jenny. Everything you ever dreamed of, they make it right here. Iron stoves, buttons, ships, shirts, hairbrushes, paint, steam engines, books. A sewer system make your eyes bug out. Oh, this is a city, all right. 45 If you have to live in a city – this is it.'

The Bodwins lived right in the center of a street full of houses and trees. Mr Garner leaped out and tied his horse to a solid iron post.

'Here we are.' 50

Baby picked up her bundle and with great difficulty, caused by her hip and the hours of sitting in a wagon, climbed down. Mr Garner was up the walk and on the porch before she touched ground, but she got a peep at a Negro girl's face at the open door before she followed 55 a path to the back of the house. She waited what seemed a long time before this same girl opened the kitchen door and offered her a seat by the window.

'Can I get you anything to eat, ma'am?' the girl asked.

'No, darling. I'd look favorable on some water though.' 60 The girl went to the sink and pumped a cupful of water. She placed it in Baby Suggs' hand. 'I'm Janey, ma'am.'

Baby, marveling at the sink, drank every drop of water although it tasted like a serious medicine. 'Suggs,' she said, blotting her lips with the back of her hand. 'Baby Suggs.' 65

'Glad to meet you, Mrs Suggs. You going to be staying here?'

'I don't know where I'll be. Mr Garner – that's him what brought me here – he say he arrange something for me.' And then, 'I'm free, you know.'   70

Making History: Brian Friel

LOMBARD It's been a difficult time for you, Hugh. That's why this history is important – is vitally important. These last years have been especially frustrating. But what we must remember – what I must record and celebrate – is the *whole* life,   5
from the very beginning right through those glorious years when aspiration and achievement came together and O'Neill was a household name right across Europe. Because they were glorious, Hugh. And they are a cause for celebration not   10
only by us but by the generations that follow us. Now. (*Finds his outline.*) I think this is it – is it? Yes, it is.

O'NEILL Mabel will be in the history, Peter?

LOMBARD Mabel? What sort of a question is that? Of   15
course Mabel will be in the history.

O'NEILL Central to it, Peter.

LOMBARD And so will your first wife, Brian MacFelim's daughter. And so will your second, the wonderful Siobhan. And so will Mabel. And so will our   20
beautiful Catriona – she says not to wait up for her. They'll all be mentioned. What a strange question! (*Confidentially*) But I've got to confess a secret unease, Hugh. The fact that the great Hugh

O'Neill had four wives – and there were rumours   25
of a fifth years and years ago, weren't there? –
long before you and I first met – but the fact that
O'Neill had four, shall we say acknowledged, wives,
do you think that may strike future readers as
perhaps... a surfeit? I'm sure not. I'm sure I'm being   30
too sensitive. Anyhow we can't deliberately suppress
what we know did happen, can we? So. Back to
my overall framework.

O'NEILL This is my last battle, Peter.

LOMBARD Battle? What battle?   35

O'NEILL That [*book*].

LOMBARD What are you talking about?

O'NEILL That thing there.

LOMBARD Your history?

O'NEILL *Your* history. I'm an old man. I have no posi-   40
tion, no power, no money. No, I'm not whingeing –
I'm not pleading. But I'm telling you that
I'm going to fight you on that and I'm going to win.

LOMBARD Fight – ? What in the name of God is the
man talking about?   45

O'NEILL I don't trust you. I don't trust you to tell the
truth.

LOMBARD To tell the truth in – ? Do you really think I
would – ?

O'NEILL I think you are not trustworthy. And that [*book*]   50
is all that is left to me.

LOMBARD You *are* serious! Hugh, for heaven's sake – !
Lombard bursts out laughing.

O'NEILL Go ahead. Laugh. But I'm going to win this
battle, Peter.

LOMBARD Hold on now – wait – wait – wait – wait. Just   55
tell me one thing. Is this book some sort of a malign
scheme? Am I doing something reprehensible?

O'NEILL You are going to embalm me in – in – in a florid lie.

LOMBARD Will I lie, Hugh?   60

O'NEILL I need the truth, Peter. That's all that's left. The schemer, the leader, the liar, the statesman, the lecher, the patriot, the drunk, the soured, bitter émigré – put it *all* in, Peter. Record the *whole* life – that's what you said yourself.   65

LOMBARD Listen to me, Hugh –

O'NEILL I'm asking you, man. Yes, damn it, I am pleading. Don't embalm me in pieties.

LOMBARD Let me tell you what I'm doing.

O'NEILL You said Mabel will have her place. That place   70
is central to me.

LOMBARD Will you listen to me?

O'NEILL Can I trust you to make Mabel central?

An Evil Cradling: Brian Keenan

The butt was lifted, and he stood exhausted and panting above me. The smell of him, his sweet sickly perfume, the sweat, the garlic from his panting breath repelled me. The room was pungent with his violent aroma. I wanted him to leave, not because I was afraid of him,   5
but because this man had violated me with a rifle butt and I wanted every trace of him and the air in which he stood sucked out of that cell. His presence was being pushed down my throat and I could not abide it. The anger in me became a volcano in my chest and if I   10
trembled now, I trembled with a subdued fury. It was an elemental anger and had nothing to do with who or what I was or that personality I had insisted on maintaining

for myself. This was a rage that was greater than me. How long could I contain myself? The blows and the bruises and the kicks hurt me but I felt no pain, just this cold anger. And as I felt it gather up its force in me and move towards the moment when it would explode, Said was gone.

The banging door confirmed it. But cautious that he might be standing there, I waited. I sniffed the air like an animal. His smell lingered but it was less strong. He had gone. I slowly lifted up my blindfold and looked at John, he looked at me. We could not see much in the darkness. 'Are you all right?' he asked. 'Yes,' I said and winked. For a few moments we were shocked and too frightened to speak. Then slowly crawling through the darkness towards one another, we felt each other's arms and faces. 'Are you sore?' 'Not really.' 'No, I'm not either but I expect we'll feel it in the morning.' Our voices were now very, very low. We could hardly hear each other speaking. We whispered soft words of comfort and reassurance to each other. 'The man's a fucking head banger! He is a wank-stain, an empty piece of exhausted flesh.'

We both lay back in the dark to calm ourselves and flush out the arrogance of his violence. I thought, as the anger began to ebb back in great torrents, how I would take great pleasure in castrating that man and quietly standing over him as I watched him and made him eat himself. I spat out my anger in silent and foul abuse. This man had ceased to have any element of humanity. I could not consider him human. Twice now he had beaten me and sought to humiliate me and I wondered how many more times before I could contain myself no longer and try to wreak havoc on him. I remembered as I lay there how he had often quoted a phrase from the Koran, one that is copied from the Christian Bible. 'An eye for an eye and a tooth for a tooth.'

As my anger diminished I felt a new and tremendous   50
kind of strength flooding me. The more I was beaten the stronger I seemed to become. It was not strength of arm, nor of body but a huge determination never to give in to these men, never to show fear, never to cower in front of them. To take what violence they meted out   55
to me and stand and resist and not allow myself to be humiliated. In that resistance I would humiliate them. There was a part of me they could never bind nor abuse nor take from me. There was a sense of self greater than me alone, which came and filled me in the darkest hours.   60

Introduction to *Six Women Poets*: Grace Nichols

As a writer and poet I'm excited by language of course. I care about language, and maybe that is another reason why I write. It's the battle with language that I love, that striving to be true to the inner language of my voice, the challenge of trying to create something new. I like   5
working in both Standard English and Creole. I tend to want to fuse the two tongues because I come from a background where the two worlds were constantly interacting, though Creole was regarded, obviously, as the inferior by the colonial powers when I was   10
growing up.

I think this is one of the main reasons why many Caribbean poets, including myself, have reclaimed our language heritage and are now exploring it. It's a language

our foremothers and forefathers struggled to create after   15
losing their own languages on the plantations and we
are saying it's a valid, vibrant language. We're no longer
going to treat it with contempt or allow it to be
misplaced. We just don't see Creole as a dialect of
English even though the words themselves are English-   20
based, because the structure, rhythm, and intonation are
an influence of West African speech.

As someone from the Caribbean, I feel very multi-
cultural and have been affected by all the different
strands in that culture – African, Amerindian, Asian,   25
European. I have a natural fear of anything that tries to
close in on me, whether it is an ideology or a group of
people who feel that we should all think alike because
we're all women or because we're all black, and there is
no room to accommodate anyone with a different view.   30
In the early days when I first started reading my poems,
mostly from *Long-memoried Woman*, a few women
wanted to know why I wasn't focusing on the 'realities'
of black women in this country – racial discrimination,
bad housing etc. There is a great danger of stereotyping   35
and limiting the lives of black people if we only see
them as 'sufferers'. The poem, *Of course when they ask
for poems about the Realities of black women*, affirms their
complexity.

Captain Corelli's Mandolin: Louis de Bernières

L' Omosessuale (1)

I, Carlo Piero Guercio, write these words with the intention that they should be found after my death, when neither scorn nor loss of reputation may dog my steps nor blemish me. The circumstance of life leaves it impossible that this testament of my nature should find its way into the world before I have drawn my last breath, and until that time I shall be condemned to wear the mask decreed by misfortune.

I have been reduced to eternal and infinite silence, I have not even told the chaplain in confession. I know in advance what I will be told; that it is a perversion, an abomination in the sight of God, that I must fight the good fight, that I must marry and lead the life of a normal man, that I have a choice.

I have not told a doctor. I know in advance that I will be called an invert, that I am in some strange way in love with myself, that I am sick and can be cured, that my mother is responsible, that I am an effeminate even though I am as strong as an ox and fully capable of lifting my own weight above my head, that I must marry and lead the life of a normal man, that I have a choice.

What could I say to such priests and doctors? I would say to the priest that God made me as I am, that I had no choice, that He must have made me like this for a purpose, that He knows the ultimate reasons for all things and that therefore it must be all to the good that I am as I am, even if we cannot know what that good is. I can say to the priest that if God is the reason for

all things, then God is to blame and I should not be
condemned.   30

And the priest will say, 'This is a matter of the Devil
and not of God,' and I will reply, 'Did God not make
the Devil? Is He not omniscient? How can I be blamed
for what He knew would occur from the very commence-
ment of time?' And the priest will refer me to the   35
destruction of Sodom and Gomorrah and tell me that
God's mysteries are not to be understood by us. He will
tell me that we are commanded to be fruitful and
multiply.

I would say to the doctor, 'I have been like this from   40
the first, it is nature that has moulded me, how am I
supposed to change? How can I decide to desire women,
any more than I can suddenly decide to enjoy eating
anchovies, which I have always detested? I have been to
the Casa Rosetta, and I loathed it, and afterwards I felt   45
sick. I felt cheapened. I felt I was a traitor. I had to do
it to appear normal.'

And the doctor will say, 'How can this be natural?
Nature serves its interests by making us reproduce. This
is against nature. Nature wants us to be fruitful and   50
multiply.'

This is a conspiracy of doctors and priests who repeat
the same things in different words. It is medicinal
theology and theological medicine. I am like a spy who
has signed a covenant of perpetual secrecy, I am like   55
someone who is the only person in the world that knows
the truth and yet is forbidden to utter it. And this truth
weighs more than the universe, so that I am like Atlas
bowed down forever beneath a burden that cracks the
bones and solidifies the blood. There is no air in this   60
world that I am fated to inhabit, I am a plant suffocated

by lack of air and light, I have had my roots clipped and
my leaves painted with poison. I am exploding with the
fire of love and there is no one to accept it or nourish
it. I am a foreigner within my own nation, an alien in   65
my own race, I am as detested as cancer when I am as
purely flesh as any priest or doctor.

Little Red-Cap: Carol Ann Duffy

At childhood's end, the houses petered out
into playing fields, the factory, allotments
kept, like mistresses, by kneeling married men,
the silent railway line, the hermit's caravan,
till you came at last to the edge of the woods.   5
It was there that I first clapped eyes on the wolf.

He stood in a clearing, reading his verse out loud
in his wolfy drawl, a paperback in his hairy paw,
red wine staining his bearded jaw. What big ears
he had! What big eyes he had! What teeth!   10
In the interval, I made quite sure he spotted me,
sweet sixteen, never been, babe, waif, and bought me a
    drink,

my first. You might ask why. Here's why. Poetry.
The wolf, I knew, would lead me deep into the woods,
away from home, to a dark tangled thorny place   15
lit by the eyes of owls. I crawled in his wake,
my stockings ripped to shreds, scraps of red from my blazer
snagged on twig and branch, murder clues. I lost both
    shoes

but got there, wolf's lair, better beware. Lesson one that
   night,
breath of the wolf in my ear, was the love poem.   20
I clung till dawn to his thrashing fur, for
what little girl doesn't dearly love a wolf?
Then I slid from between his heavy matted paws
and went in search of a living bird – white dove –

which flew, straight, from my hands to his open mouth.   25
One bite, dead. How nice, breakfast in bed, he said,
licking his chops. As soon as he slept, I crept to the back
of the lair, where a whole wall was crimson, gold, aglow
   with books.
Words, words were truly alive on the tongue, in the
   head,
warm, beating, frantic, winged; music and blood.   30

But then I was young – and it took ten years
in the woods to tell that a mushroom
stoppers the mouth of a buried corpse, that birds
are the uttered thought of trees, that a greying wolf
howls the same old song at the moon, year in, year out, 35
season after season, same rhyme, same reason. I took
   an axe

to a willow to see how it wept. I took an axe to a salmon
to see how it leapt. I took an axe to the wolf
as he slept, one chop, scrotum to throat, and saw
the glistening, virgin white of my grandmother's bones. 40
I filled his old belly with stones. I stitched him up.
Out of the forest I come with my flowers, singing, all
   alone.

Knowing Me: Benjamin Zephaniah

According to de experts
I'm letting my side down,
Not playing the alienation game,
It seems I am too unfrustrated.
I have refused all counselling   5
I refuse to appear on daytime television
On night-time documentaries,
I'm not longing and yearning.
I don't have an identity crisis.

As I drive on poetic missions   10
On roads past midnight
I am regularly stopped by officers of the law
Who ask me to identify myself.
At times like these I always look into the mirror
Point   15
And politely assure them that
What I see is me.
I don't have an identity crisis.

I have never found the need
To workshop dis matter,   20
Or sit with fellow poets exorcising ghosts
Whilst searching for soulmates.
I don't wonder what will become of me
If I don't eat reggae food or dance to mango tunes,
Or think of myself as a victim of circumstance. 25
I'm the dark man, black man
With a brown dad, black man
Mommy is a red skin, black woman,
She don't have an identity crisis.

Being black somewhere else   30
Is just being black everywhere,
I don't have an identity crisis.
At least once a week I watch television
With my Jamaican hand on my Ethiopian heart
The African heart deep in my Brummie chest,   35
And I chant, Aston Villa, Aston Villa, Aston Villa,
Believe me I know my stuff.
I am not wandering drunk into the rootless future
Nor am I going back in time to find somewhere to live.
I just don't want to live in a field with my past   40
Looking at blades of grass that look just like me, near
    a relic like me
Where the thunder is just like me, talking to someone
    just like me,
I don't just want to love me and only me; diversity is
    my pornography,
I want to make politically aware love with the rainbow.
Check dis Workshop Facilitator   45
Dis is me.
I don't have an identity crisis.

I have reached the stage where I can recognise my
    shadow.
I'm quite pleased with myself.
When I'm sunbathing in Wales   50
I can see myself in India
As clearly as I see myself in Mexico.
I have now reached the stage
Where I am sick of people asking me if I feel British
    or West Indian,
African or Black, Dark and Lonely, Confused or Patriotic.   55
The thing is I don't feel lost,

I didn't even begin to look for myself until I met a social
   worker
And a writer looking for a subject
Nor do I write to impress poets.
Dis is not an emergency   60
I'm as kool as my imagination, I'm care more than your
   foreign policy.
I don't have an identity crisis.

I don't need an identity crisis to be creative,
I don't need an identity crisis to be oppressed.
I need love warriors and free minds wherever they are,   65
I need go getters and wide awakers for rising and shining,
I need to know that I can walk into any temple
Rave at any rave
Or get the kind of justice that my folk can see is just.
I am not half a poet shivering in the cold   70
Waiting for a culture shock to warm my longlost drum
   rhythm,
I am here and now, I am all that Britain is about
I'm happening as we speak.
Honestly,
I don't have an identity crisis.   75

Spies: Michael Frayn

There were many things that Keith had been wrong
about, I realised gradually as life went on. But about one
thing, and one quite surprising thing, he'd been right,
though it took me several years to recognise it. There
was a German spy in the Close that summer. It wasn't   5
his mother – it was me.

Everything is as it was; and everything has changed. Stephen Wheatley has become this old man, treading slowly and warily in the footsteps of his former self, and the name of this old man is Stefan Weitzler. That undersized observer in the privet, spying on the comings and goings of the street, has reverted to the name under which he was registered in the peaceful green district of the great German city where he was born.

I was reborn as Stephen when my parents left Germany in 1935. My mother was English anyway, and she'd always spoken English to us at home, but now my father became more English still, and we all turned into Wheatleys. She died at the beginning of the 1960s, and when my father followed her less than a year later I felt a great restlessness stirring in me – the converse of that same restlessness that's brought me back now to the Close. It's the longing to be elsewhere that in Germany we call *Fernweh*, which is in my case also *Heimweh*, a longing to be home – the terrible pull of opposites that torments the displaced everywhere.

Well, my life in England had somehow never really taken flight. My marriage was never quite a real marriage, my job in the engineering department of the local polytechnic was never quite a real job. I felt a yearning to know more about my father, about where he'd grown up, where he and my mother had fallen in love, where I'd first seen the light. So I went to take a look, and I discovered that my first two years had been spent in a quiet, garden-lined street that seemed to be a dreamlike echo of the Close in which I later grew up, which is no doubt why the Close itself always seemed to be a dreamlike echo in its turn.

I had a bleak few months in my rediscovered homeland, struggling with a language I'd only started to learn in my adolescence, too late to be ever quite at ease with, working in an environment I couldn't quite understand. Of my father's past scarcely a trace remained. His parents and two brothers had all been taken and murdered. His sister had for some reason been left, and instead had been killed in her own cellar, along with her two children, by Uncle Peter, or by his colleagues in Bomber Command.

And yet, and yet… I stayed. My temporary job somehow became a permanent one. I don't suppose you've ever read the English-language installation and maintenance manuals for Siemens transformers and high-voltage switchgear, but if by any chance you have then you're familiar with at any rate some of my work. The story in the manuals, it occurs to me, is once again somebody else's, just as the story of the German spy, and all the other stories of my childhood, were Keith's. Once again all I've done is play the loyal disciple.

And of course the day came when I met someone else, and as I began to see Germany through her familiar eyes, my perception of everything around me changed once again… Soon there was a house, in another quiet, tree-lined street… The house became a home… There were children, and many German in-laws to visit… And now, before I can sort out whether I belong here or there, or even which is here and which is there, my children are grown up, and we have their mother's grave to tend each week.

Late Spring: Owen Sheers

It made me feel like a man
when I helped my grandfather
castrate the early lambs –

picking the hard orange O-rings
from the plastic bag   5
and stretching them across the made-to-purpose
   tool,

heavy and steel-hard in the sun,
while he turned one between his legs
to play it like a cello.

Spreading the pink unwooled skin at their groins   10
he'd coax them up into the sack,
one-handed, like a man milking,

two soaped beans into a delicate purse,
while gesturing with his other
for the tool, a pliers in reverse,   15

which I'd pass to him then stand and stare
as he let his clenched fist open
to crown them.

We did the tails too while we were there
so when I walked the field weeks later,   20
both could be counted;

the tails scattered like catkins among
the windfall of our morning's work –
a strange harvest of the seeds we'd sown.

Mr Pip: Lloyd Jones

But he did have something new to share.

Looking around at our smiling faces, he must have adjudged there to be no finer or more appropriate moment than the present one. He touched his collar button. The white of his suit shone in the light from the fire.

'My darling Grace gave me great happiness,' he said. 'None greater than when she gave me a child, a baby girl to whom we gave the name Sarah.'

Mr Watts stopped here, but it wasn't the usual pause for me to pass on what he had said. It was so he could collect himself. He stared into the night high above the flames of the fire.

Everyone saw him swallow, and our silence deepened.

He nodded up at that baby girl. He smiled away, and we smiled with him. He almost laughed, and we were ready to laugh too when he said, 'We could not stop looking at her. We stood by the rail of her cot, looking down at her face.' He nodded at the memory, then looked at his audience. 'By the way, this is how white turns mulatto and black white. If you are the blaming kind, blame it on the horizon.' Those who got the point laughed; some of the rambos followed suit out of fear they had missed something.

Mr Watts continued.

'I have told you I came into this world an orphaned boy. I have no memory of my parents. I have no photographs. I have no idea what they looked like. But in that baby's face I thought I saw my dead parents emerge. I saw my mother's eyes, my father's cleft chin. I remember standing at the rail of the cot, staring with the hungry

eyes of an explorer seeing new territory for the first
time. It was familiar geography all muddled up. I saw
bits and pieces of Anglo-Welsh heritage in a coffee-
coloured skin. Between us, me and Grace had created a   35
new world.'

I liked that idea. It encouraged me to think about my
father. Perhaps he wasn't lost. Or we weren't lost.

If I'd owned a mirror I would have peered in it for a
trace of my lost father. The still pools up in the hill   40
streams did not offer the same detail. My face shim-
mered and darkened. So I sat on a rock and moved my
fingers around my face. I thought I might find some tell-
tale trace of my dad there.

My father had a rubbery mouth – from all that fat   45
laughter of his, I guess. My lips were thinner, like my
mum's, sharpened from making judgments. I traced my
eyes but they just felt like my eyes. I found my ears. I
have large ears and I will never lose them. They are
listening ears. According to my mum, my dad had only   50
ever used his to listen to his own booming laughter.

I decided that if I carried a trace of my dad it lay
deeper than on the surface of things, maybe it circulated
in the heart, or in the head wherever memory collects.
And I thought I would sacrifice any physical likeness   55
for the hope that he had not forgotten me, his daughter
Matilda, wherever he was out there in the white world.

Notes

A Doll's House: Henrik Ibsen (1879)

Norwegian poet and dramatist Henrik Ibsen (1828–1906) published *A Doll's House* in 1879. It is perhaps his most controversial work, springing from his belief that husband and wife should live as equals, and his concern for the rights of women in a male-dominated society. In this society, women only had status as wives and mothers once they eased away from the role of child and left the care of their parents.

In the play, Nora lives the life of the doll in its title, subject to her husband's whims and constraints. His names for her, such as *songbird*, *little spendthrift* and *skylark* suggest role-playing, and she has indeed been playing the role of wife and mother in her life with Torvald Helmer. However, she has secretly taken out a loan for the sake of her husband, who at the play's climax angrily berates her for damaging his honour and reputation. What she did was in fact illegal: women were not allowed to have loans at the time. When he realizes that they are *saved* as no one will know, he forgives rather than thanks his wife, stating: *There is something so indescribably sweet and satisfying to a man in the knowledge that he has forgiven his wife... It seems as if he has made her... doubly his own*. He adds that he has given her *new life so to speak*, and she has become in a way both wife and child to him. He refers to Nora as his *little scared helpless darling*.

It is at this point that she feels it is time for her to assert her individuality as woman, not a doll-wife to Helmer and mother to his children.

In this extract, almost at the end of the play, Nora tells him that they have never understood each other and that this is the time for *the settling of accounts*.

Nora's struggle to find her own identity is one that she seeks to undergo without Helmer's or anyone else's aid, and there is bravery in her decision to stand alone, leaving the family home to pursue that aim. At the time when these lines were written, this was brave indeed and the play caused uproar because of its ending.

The form of this extract is interesting, consisting as it does of a series of questions by Helmer and answers from Nora, suggesting perhaps a shift in the balance of power in their relationship.

2–3 **we two, you and I, husband and wife** Nora's repetition here of three different ways of referring to herself and Helmer suggests the intensity with which she is seeking to establish a sense of identity.

16–18 **I have been greatly wronged... first by Papa and then by you** for most of her life Nora has been treated in a way that has not been beneficial.

29 **his doll child** echoes the play's title, and her reference to herself as Helmer's *doll wife* (line 53) with her own children carrying on the doll dynasty as her *dolls*. This central image is potent, suggesting as it does the idea of being diminutive – and perhaps hence subordinate – and more particularly having no control. Dolls are controlled by others, are silent and express no views, and do nothing of their own volition. This is how Nora sees herself. This has been her identity for the whole of her life.

52–3 **But our home has been nothing but a playroom** the idea of playing is interesting, suggesting that nothing in her life has been serious or real, that it has all been role-playing and games. The repetition of the idea of play and dolls is central to this extract. Nora perceives herself, in this epiphanic moment, as a person whose identity has been subordinated to first her father, then her husband.

60–1 **Playtime shall be over and lesson time shall begin** it is deeply ironic that Helmer, in reply to the speech about having *fun*, asserts somewhat patronizingly that *playtime* will be succeeded by *lessons*, continuing the idea of his wife as his subordinate – he is the teacher, she the pupil.

63 **Both yours and the children's, my darling Nora** this compounds the insult, lumping her together with the children

as if equally in need of his educative powers. It also furthers the idea that Nora is a child and that she is not a person in her own right. Notice too the use of the proprietorial personal pronoun *my*.

75 **I must try and educate myself**   this neatly repudiates Helmer's claim to be her teacher.

79–80 **I must stand quite alone if I am to understand myself and everything about me**   this repudiates any claim on her by Helmer and is a bold statement about her independence.

The House of Bernarda Alba: Federico García Lorca (1936)

Written in 1936 as part of a 'rural trilogy', shortly before the author was killed by supporters of General Franco, the Spanish fascist dictator, this play was not performed until 1945.

The house of the title is that of Bernarda, who has just buried her second husband and has decreed an eight-year period of mourning, a tradition in her family. During this time her five daughters will remain isolated, even though the eldest, Angustias, is engaged to Pepe from the local village.

Angustias is 39, sickly and rich; her father, Bernarda's first husband, left her a fortune. Her sisters, daughters of the now-deceased Antonio Maria Benavides, are Magdalena (30), Amelia (27), Martirio (24) and 20-year-old Adela. Poncia is the housekeeper.

Bernarda's strict ruling of her household (symbolized by her cane) is cruel and unwavering. None of her daughters has any freedom or the ability to be herself. All must conform and live as isolated virgins until the mourning period is over.

Meanwhile, Angustias speaks to her fiancé through the window, Martirio falls hopelessly in love with him, and Adela, the youngest, conducts a passionate affair with him unknown to her mother.

At the play's climax, when passions reach their height and Martirio and Adela can no longer bear their mother's suppression of their natural instincts, they struggle for supremacy as rivals for Pepe.

Bernarda, enraged, rushes out of the house, a shot is heard and Pepe flees. Adela, consumed with grief, commits suicide and her mother, preoccupied with family honour and her good name, asserts a new identity for her by claiming that she died a virgin.

At the beginning of this extract, which brings the play to its conclusion, Martirio and Adela reveal the truth about themselves to each other.

1 **He loves me, *me*!**   Adela's intensity is shown here by her exclamatory tone, the repetition of *me* and its italicization, and the further repetition of the whole phrase. She can at last assert her identity as the lover of Pepe. For the whole of the play this has been kept secret.

10–11 **because you too love him! You love him!**   Adela's intensity is shown again and results in her sister's confession.

13–14 **My breast's bitter, bursting like a pomegranate**   Martirio's explosive 'b' sounds add weight to the enormity of her confession. Like Adela she is at last able to reveal the truth about herself and bring an end to her mother's suppression.

15 sd *hugging her*   the stage direction shows Adela attempting to create a feeling of sisterhood, previously impossible, rather than rivalry with Martirio.

18–20 **My blood's no longer yours… I see you as just another woman**   Martirio denies the bonds of sisterhood. Adela no longer qualifies as a sister and has become like any rival.

21–2 **Whoever has to drown – let her drown**   the motif of drowning implies that now Adela too sees the end of sisterhood. Each of them is alone.

25–6 **I can't stand this horrible house after the taste of his mouth**   Adela is shown to be a sensuous woman who is now struggling against her mother's bonds.

29–31 **the crown of thorns that belongs to the mistress of a married man**   this biblical image shows the intensity of Adela's desire to be anything but the trapped daughter of Bernarda. The identity of mistress is preferable, even if she becomes an object of scorn like Christ on his way to the cross.

47 **I can see you as I've never seen you before**   this implies that like Adela, Martirio has taken on a new role, or that at last Adela sees her as she really is, also passionately in love with Pepe to the exclusion of all else.

56–7 **She was with him. Look at those skirts covered with straw**! Martirio, as she claimed earlier, is viewing her sister as *another woman* when she graphically identifies Adela as Pepe's lover.

61 sd *Adela snatches away her mother's cane and breaks it in two* the stage direction shows a shocking and symbolic moment. Bernarda's power is broken, ironically, by her youngest daughter, who is asserting her right to independence and an end to tyranny.

63 **No one but Pepe commands me**   when Adela exclaims this, she is putting an end to her mother's rule. Ironically she is putting herself under the command of another, this time Pepe.

65–7 **I'm his… He'll be master in this house**   Adela passes herself to Pepe's control. The house, too, changes its identity, reminding us of the play's title.

68–74 **My God!… never see her again!**   the short, staccato statements and exclamations signal the breakdown in order and the collapse of sisterly feeling.

76–7 **That does away with Pepe el Romano**   Martirio is shown at her most spiteful. Adela rushes out defeated, thinking her lover is dead, and hence her identity as his mistress. But Martirio knows that he escaped Bernarda's shot.

103 **Cut her down!**   this instruction makes it clear that Adela has hanged herself.

My daughter died a virgin   this re-establishes Adela's identity as chaste and untouched by a man. Bernarda's lie reasserts the sham that is the family's honour.

112–13 **We'll drown ourselves in a sea of mourning**   this continues the motif of being entirely overwhelmed by mourning as if there are so many tears that they become like a sea. No one will be able to break away and perform an individual act.

115 **Silence!**   the last word of the play. It is a command to the daughters to be complicit in their mother's lie.

The Glass Menagerie: Tennessee Williams (1945)

Tennessee Williams (1911–1983) was born in Mississippi in the US. His father was a travelling salesman who moved the family to St Louis, where he and his sister had difficulties in settling. Williams left his college place to work as a clerk in a shoe company while writing in the evenings. Later he went to Iowa University and received a Rockefeller Fellowship for his play *Battle of Angels* in 1941. He went on to write a large number of plays. *The Glass Menagerie* was copyrighted in 1945 and published along with *A Streetcar Named Desire* in 1959.

The play centres on three members of the Wingfield family. Amanda is the mother of the reclusive Laura (the owner of the collection of glass animals to which the title refers) and Tom, an aspiring writer, whose clerical job in a shoe factory pays the rent.

Tension between the family members centres chiefly on Amanda and Tom; she tries to control him and he has to struggle against her to lead his own life outside their home. Amanda has been brought up as a 'Southern Belle', has married unwisely and has been left by her husband, who is described as being *in love with long distances*. Her greatest desire is to see her children happily married and prosperous, and she frequently dreams of her past life in Blue Mountain where she was surrounded by 'gentleman callers'.

Tom, sometimes irritated by his mother's dwelling on her past, actively opposes what he sees as his mother's stifling control, and in this scene his writing (as indicated by the stage directions), his interest in reading modern literature, and his desire to *go every night to the movies* all cause his mother to be exasperated.

As Tom struggles to assert himself and to gain an identity separate from that of son and breadwinner, his mother becomes increasingly theatrical in her opposition to him. It is as if she is playing a part, while he struggles to be himself.

The opening lines of the extract vividly portray his struggle even to finish a sentence.

1–6 **What in Christ's name... out of your senses**   this antiphonal exchange, in which a statement is only completed after the beginning of another, is partly humorous but also highly serious.

10–12 **I've got *no thing*... I can call my OWN**   the italics, repetition and capitals indicate how much stress Tom places on these words and hence how important it is to him to be able to own something himself as an individual.

17 **I took that horrible novel back to the library**   this shows how much Amanda interferes in her son's life.

18–21 **hideous... insane... diseased minds... FILTH**   Amanda's hyperbole in describing D.H. Lawrence's work is comic.

22 **No.... no!**   Amanda is almost hysterical.

23 **Who pays rent on it**   Tom's rhetorical question shows up the contradiction in their situation. He is being treated like a child but is in fact the breadwinner.

28 **I don't want to hear any more!**   Tom does not succeed in completing a statement until he says this, and he takes action, tearing open the portières (gauze-like screens) which separate the two of them from the audience. How do you respond to the stage directions which follow?

30 **No, I won't hear more, I'm going out**   this is Tom's final rejection of his mother's control and an assertion of his own will as an autonomous adult.

All My Sons: Arthur Miller (1947)

Arthur Miller (1915–2005) was an important figure in American literature for many decades. He was a prolific writer of plays, of which *All My Sons* is one of the most famous and was the first to be performed. He also wrote screenplays (notably *The Misfits* in which his then wife Marilyn Monroe appeared), prose fiction and an autobiography, *Time Bends*.

Trained as a journalist originally, he became known as a radical and was caught up in the anti-communist witch hunt led by Senator Joseph McCarthy, which demanded that people named others – their fiends or colleagues – who might be communists or have communist sympathies. The hysteria and persecution of innocents that this involved led him to write *The Crucible*, based on the Salem witch trials of 1692 in New England.

All My Sons is concerned with the conflict of ideology between Joe Keller and his son Chris. Joe, a wartime profiteer who shipped out cracked cylinder heads for use in aeroplanes piloted by American servicemen, causing their deaths, claims he did it for 'the business' and thus for his son Chris. For much of he play he is unaware that his elder son Larry – supposedly missing in the war – killed himself, unable to cope with the knowledge of what his father had done. Chris's beliefs contrast with those of his father. For him, *a kind of responsibility* between men is what is important.

In the extract Chris and Ann (who was previously engaged to Larry) have met for the first time, having realized and declared their mutual love. For Chris, being the lover of 'Larry's girl' is problematic. So is life after the war, living in what he sees as a selfish society.

2 **Like Larry's brother. Do it like you, Chris**   the way Chris has just kissed Ann is not as himself, but as the brother of Larry, Ann's original fiancé. His identity as Chris is overpowered by being brother to Larry.

8–9 **there was something ashamed**   Chris is not at ease with himself.

10–11 **Yes. I suppose I have been. But it's going from me**   this implies that perhaps he is winning the struggle to be himself and unashamed.

28–9 **They didn't die; they killed themselves for each other**   what do you think he means by this? How do you respond to Chris's account of the *kid* and the *socks*?

31–3 **Everything was being destroyed... one new thing was made**   this paradox expresses Chris's emerging sense of self.

33–4 **A kind of – responsibility. Man for man. You understand me?**   Chris's hesitation before *responsibility* shows how his ideas are in the process of being formed. *Man for man* clarifies his thoughts about what he is beginning to feel.

36–8 **everyone would feel it... a difference to him (*Pause*)** this reasserts the idea of men working for each other. The pause suggests how deeply Chris has come to believe that taking responsibility is what defined his men and himself.

39–40 **there was no meaning in it here... a bus accident** the bathos here shows the difference between the attitude of people back home and the sense of responsibility Chris has experienced, and the sacrifices of the lives of his men.

41–2 **I went to work with Dad... ashamed somehow** for Chris, the role of businessman is so much at odds with his newly discovered sense of who he is that he feels shame.

44 **I felt wrong to be alive** Chris feels that his very existence is being called into question because of being once more in business.

48–9 **the love a man can have for a man, you've got to be a little better** Chris is aware of the difference in morality between the new sense of responsibility he feels as a result of his war experiences and those people at home who have not altered.

50–1 **Otherwise what you have... I didn't want to take any of it** Chris is rejecting his father's values (making money) and thus creating a new sense of who he is, a man with a sense of responsibility to others.

The Go-Between: L.P. Hartley (1953)

Born in 1895, Leslie Poles Hartley was principally a reviewer of other writers' fiction for 30 years. His first novel was published in 1944 and arguably his most famous one, *The Go-Between*, in 1953 – almost the middle of the twentieth century. Interestingly, the text focuses on the shift from the previous (the nineteenth) century to the new one.

The idea of being on the cusp is central to the text; it focuses on the change from one century with an old, class-based set of values to the next, in which – with the outbreak of the First World War – those values will be displaced. This forms a parallel with the development of the protagonist, Leo, a 12-year-old who is leaving childhood and poised on the edge of adulthood. Leo is the 'go-between' of the title, carrying letters between illicit lovers, whom he thinks are no more than friends. He is eager to understand the world of adults but very confused by it, and misreads or misunderstands situations and relationships in his struggle to gain a sense of self. By the end of the novel, when he is an old man, this has still eluded him.

In this extract Leo, who narrates the text retrospectively, has just turned 13 and is considering who he is, boy or man, and the roles he has played in the past. He presents these in a list of things he now disparages. His conclusion that they were the actions of someone else suggests that a rite of passage has been negotiated. Leo is no longer the boy he was, but a young man embarking on the first phases of adulthood.

The conceptualization here – as well as the use of what one might consider an advanced vocabulary for a 13-year-old – can be attributed to the fact that the Leo who is the narrator in the 'now' of the text is an old man.

The extract is interesting in suggesting that a false sense of being an adult can be harmful.

1 **Now that I was thirteen**   Leo is marked out as a teenager – a concept which was foreign to the time in which the story is set. Nevertheless, what follows makes it clear he is no longer a child.

1–2 **I was under an obligation to look reality in the face**   this suggests that the time for fantasy is over.

4 **last night's performance**   this refers to Leo's attempts to demolish the deadly nightshade plant in the outhouse of the house in which he is a guest.

6 **my career as a magician**   Leo had been interested in magic spells, hence the reference to *mumbo-jumbo*.

13 **I condemned them unheard**   Leo's rejection of his past activities is uncompromising.

17–18 **Jenkins and Strode**   two boys at Leo's school.

18–20 **I had been playing a part, which seemed to have taken in everybody**   Leo views himself as being a kind of actor in life rather than living it.

22–3 **a tendency to ape an alien personality**   this suggests the idea of claiming a false identity.

23–6 **She had no objection… provided you could say *who* you were** this explanation of Leo's nurse's attitude to pretending and role-playing implies that a line is being drawn.

27–30 **if the assumed personality was a distortion… she was down on one**   this clarifies the point. Only completely transparent role-playing will do.

30–3 **Who are you being… I don't like him**   what is your response to this dialogue?

34–5 **I had been another little boy**   Leo was playing the role of *somebody one would like to be thought to be* (lines 29–30) rather than being himself.

36–9 **They like to think of a little boy… not a Leo or a Marcus** Marcus is his friend. What is your reading of this sentence?

42 **Lord Trimingham**   a friend of the family with whom Leo is staying.

43–5 **there are other ways… to make one feel unreal**   Leo had lost his sense of self, of who he was, during his visit.

45–7 **No little boy likes… treated as a little man**   what is your response to this?

47 **Marian**   the sister of Marcus, engaged to Trimingham.

48–51 **she had endowed me… had puffed me up**   this implies that Marian has done Leo a disservice, and that he might have seemed grown up but in fact was not. Being *puffed up* suggests the idea of having an inflated sense of one's own significance.

The Thought-Fox: Ted Hughes (1957)

Edward James (Ted) Hughes was Poet Laureate from 1984 until his death in 1998. Born in 1930, he was famous as a poet and as a children's writer, and was married from 1956–1963 to Sylvia Plath, the American poet. Her suicide in 1963 prompted many feminists to revile Hughes, as they claimed he was responsible for her death.

Nevertheless, Hughes avoided joining any debate about his wife or her state of mind, and was much loved and lauded for his work. When he died, fellow poet Seamus Heaney said at his funeral: 'No death in my lifetime has hurt poets more. He was a tower of tenderness and strength, a great arch under which the least of children's poetry could enter and feel secure… By his death, the veil of poetry is rent and the walls of learning broken.' This tribute attests to the high regard in which Hughes was held by his contemporary poets.

The Thought-Fox is from *The Hawk in the Rain*, a 1957 collection, and it is a poem about writing a poem. In it he suggests that the identity of the poet is subsumed by or secondary to poetic inspiration, which arrives in his head rather like a fox covering a clearing and entering its den. This analogy is central to understanding the poem and what it is saying about the writer and his or her work.

The poem begins with the writer alone with a blank page. By the end of the poem this is miraculously *printed*, both by the paw marks made by the fox and the writing of the poet.

The crafting of the poem, however, with its frequent use of enjambement, caesura, alliteration (for example in *midnight moment*, line 1) and assonance (*Between trees*, line 14) belies the idea of inspiration taking over the poet. He has clearly crafted it in a precise and meticulous way, similar to the way in which the fox-in-his-thoughts moves: *delicately* (line 9).

   1 **I imagine**   this makes clear that the scene which follows is a product of the poet's mind.

   2 This suggests that inspiration, embodied in the fox, is taking shape as if it has an identity of its own.

  3–4 These lines create a vivid impression of the writer's inability to write as yet, and of the solitary nature of his existence.

  6–8 The fox/his inspiration is approaching, seemingly without any effort on his part. The use of enjambement intensifies the sense that it is unstoppable and has taken him over.

11–13 **a movement, that now… Sets neat prints** the use of enjambement across stanzas here and later complements the idea of the fox crossing a clearing until it finds its *dark hole* (line 22), which is at the same time its den and the poet's head – the repository of the poetic idea for which it serves as a metaphor.

23–4 These details of the poet's situation return us to the start of the poem. One thing, however, has altered. As if by magic there are prints or marks of writing on the *blank page* of line 4. It is as if despite himself the poet has been visited with an inspiration that has taken him over and has produced the poem, which we the readers are now reading. The writer's identity has been subjugated by his inspiration, almost as if a part of himself has been detached in the act of creation.

Things Fall Apart: Chinua Achebe (1958)

Chinua Achebe's novel *Things Fall Apart* was, to some extent, written to present an alterative view of the people of the Congo to that given in Joseph Conrad's short novel *Heart of Darkness* (1902). Achebe's perception that Conrad's presentation belittles black people has been much discussed.

Things Fall Apart depicts the Igbo people and their English colonizers, and portrays the tragic downfall of the hero Okonkwo. His personal struggle to achieve a reputation as a fearless man and to be unlike his father results in yet more fear – of being seen to be fearful and of being like the father he despises. The result is a dishonourable death by suicide, which so disgusts fellow members of his clan that he is seen as an abomination by the tribe and becomes a footnote in a white man's history book, thus effectively erasing his identity.

The extracts (from chapters 2 and 7) focus on the male members of each generation of the hero's family: Okonkwo (the main character), his father Unoka, and his son Nwoye. A fourth male character, Ikemefuna, becomes a kind of foster son to Okonkwo and brother to Nwoye.

The first paragraph depicts Okonkwo's fatal flaw, his fearfulness of failure and weakness, which he associates with his father Unoka. His struggle is to be as unlike his father as possible. The rest introduces the young Nwoye's contrasting struggle to please his father by appearing to be like him and embracing – or pretending to embrace – his values.

1–3 **His wives… and so did his little children** this sets the tone for this important description of Okonkwo as a man who frightens his family. The word *fear* is used six more times in the following lines, but the emphasis is not on how others react to him, but on his own inner struggle not to be seen to be fearful.

5–6 **fear of failure and of weakness** this dominates his life, suggesting a man not at ease with who or what he is.

11–12 **to resemble his father** Okonkwo's struggle to be as unlike his father, Unoka, as possible pervades the text.

12–19 **resented… suffered… hate** these words make clear the strength of Okonkwo's feelings about his father. He passes these on in his dealings with his son Nwoye, who in turn is made to suffer from his father's lack of *gentleness* – a quality of Unoka that Okonkwo hates.

29 **incipient laziness** this is similar to the *idleness* attributed to Unoka, though *incipient* suggests that it is a possibility rather than a reality. Okonkwo aims to *correct* Nwoye, just the same.

29–30 **At any rate, that was how it looked to his father** this comment implies that Okonkwo's *constant nagging and beating* are unfair and the product of his obsessive need to make sure that none of his father's characteristics are handed down to the next generation.

39 **kindled a new fire** how do you respond to the details about Nwoye's behaviour as a result of Ikemefuna's influence?

41–2 **now sat with Okonkwo** this shift is symbolic, perhaps, of Nwoye's shift to adulthood and to a more overtly masculine identity, linked to tasks such as wood splitting or food pounding.

42 *obi* living quarters.

49–50 **grumble aloud about women and their troubles** this seems to be a role he is assuming on the road to becoming more manly.

53–4 **ruling his father's household** this is depicted as a manly quality.

59–60 **able to control his women-folk** as in lines 53–4 above, this suggests being firmly in charge.

60–2 **No matter… not really a man** this sentence sums up Okonkwo's view of masculine identity, an identity which Nwoye has to struggle to achieve.

64 **foo-foo** food made of starchy vegetables such as yam.

68 **to be masculine and to be violent** here manliness is seen to involve violence, which poses a dilemma for Nwoye.

69–70 **the stories that his mother used to tell** how do you respond to the details about the stories which follow?

72 *eneke-nti-oba* a kind of bird.

95 **he feigned that he no longer cared** Nwoye is denying his own identity to please his father.

The Prisoner: Amiya Rao (1960)

The anthology *Finding a Voice*, first published in 1978, looks at the experiences of a variety of Asian women in Britain who have left their homes to begin a new life. Many of the texts look at attitudes to marriage and a woman's role in the family of her parents-in-law. *The Prisoner* was translated by Amrit Wilson, the editor of the anthology, from her mother's Bengali poem written in 1960.

The first part of the poem concerns a purple and gold sari shut up in *a cheap tin trunk* unworn for years. Its owner lies dying, bringing to birth her ninth child – *with luck a son*, as daughters cost much to maintain. Her 16-year-old daughter is tempted by the beauty of the sari, which reminds her *you are sixteen only once*, but family duties overpower her. Her *miserable, ill-paid* father, her dying mother, her *battalion of young sisters and brothers* all vie for her attention and the beautiful sari remains unworn.

The central conceit of the poem – that the sari has a life of its own, and needs to be used, worn and shown – continues in the extract reproduced here. The life of the sari mirrors and keeps pace with that of the owner; it is disintegrating in the trunk, becoming pale as its owner does. The owner's identity is washed away by the pressures of never being her own person and never having had time for herself.

In this extract the 16-year-old has just been married. By the end she still has not worn the sari. Time has run out for her to enjoy life, represented by the *cuckoo* and the *trees*, and the garment is in tatters like the life of the once-vibrant woman.

3   **a man he does not know quite**   this implies that the chosen husband is almost a stranger.

4   **knotted to a stranger**   this reinforces the idea, adding the suggestion that the bonds are tight and cannot be unloosed.

6   **she accepts her destiny**   the daughter is passive, but it is also suggested that there is no choice; *destiny* implies an unavoidable fate.

7   Separated from the rest, these four words suggest the separateness of her life with her new in-laws, compared with life in her own family.

8   **under the eye... queen**   this creates a picture of surveillance.

9   **maddening jungle**   this creates an image of endless unfocused sound.

10–15   How do you respond to these lines?

17–18   The repetition of *no time* and *together* underscores the fact that the couple do not have the opportunity to enjoy each other's company – even to get to know each other – because of the demands made on them. For the husband as well as the wife a sense of identity becomes submerged under the pressures of others.

21   This is the beginning of a series of lines in which the voice of the sari moves from speaking to pleading to sobbing. The raising of the level of intensity corresponds to the passing of time.

26   **your pallor**   this is one of several references that indicate time is running out.

30   **take me out, wear me once**   this poignant line emphasizes the woman's total subservience to the demands on her time.
    time is passing   uttered by the sari sobbing, these words are repeated in the next verse paragraph by the woman, almost unwittingly. Their full force is apparent at the end of this verse paragraph when the sari's voice repeats them once more.

41   **all in tatters**   what in your view is the point of this telling detail?

Song of Lawino: Okot p'Bitek (1966)

Okot p'Bitek (1931–1982) was born in Gulu, Uganda and taught English and religious knowledge after a two-year course at teacher training college. Originally a Christian, his interests changed after a period of study at universities in England and Wales, and instead of European traditions he began studying the traditions of his own people. At Oxford he pursued this interest in working towards a degree in social anthropology, but became convinced that such study supported and justified colonialism, and he came into conflict with tutors who referred to Africans or non-Western people as 'barbarians, savages [and] primitive'.

His rejection of Western traditions is shown by his use of African forms for his poetry, as in *Song of Lawino*. This epic poem was composed while working with friends for the Gulu Festival and was read aloud as each part was written. His friends' comments were taken into consideration for possible rewritings of chapters, a method similar to the composition of traditional songs.

Song of Lawino was published originally in Luo and later translated into other languages. It is based on a real social problem. In rural East Africa it is common for men to become 'educated out of their tribe' (a comment made by Irish poet Seamus Heaney about his own situation) and to return home with altered feelings for the ways of their families.

In her *Song*, Lawino (a member of the Acholi tribe) laments the fact that her college-educated husband Ocol has turned his back on Acholi traditions in favour of Western ones and has rejected her as his wife. His second wife's attempts to westernize herself are the subject of Lawino's scorn in this extract.

The struggle for identity takes an interesting form here. Clementine (the second wife) is shaping herself to assume the identity of a Western woman. Lawino, by contrast, clings resolutely to the identity she has as an African woman, one she is proud of. Two versions of womanliness are presented here in conflict with one other.

Notes

The Woman With Whom I Share My Husband is the chapter heading for Part 2 of the poem. This statement of fact suggests that the idea of sharing is not in itself a problem. It is the woman herself that Lawino objects to.

1 **the old type**   this identifies Lawino as a traditional wife.

2–4 **a modern woman... a beautiful girl/Who speaks English** the second wife is presented as Lawino's antithesis (opposite), modern rather than of the old type, and a speaker of English like Ocol the husband.

5 **only recently**   repeated two lines later, this draws a poignant comparison between her present unhappiness and past joy.

7–9 **I would play/On my bow-harp/Singing praises to my beloved**   this presents Lawino as a wife who shows love for her husband using a traditional African instrument, in the traditional African way. Clementine by contrast does nothing, but *speaks English*.

18–19 This is the crux of the problem. Clementine, or 'Tina', is remoulding her identity. How do you respond to the description of Tina as *The beautiful one*? What tone might be used here?

20–21 This is the first of a series of comparisons which become increasingly critical.

24–5 This repellent image suggests that Tina, using lipstick to mould an identity like that of a white woman, is diseased.

34 This comparison is comic rather than disparaging, but hardly makes Tina sound like *The beautiful one*.

35 **carbolic soap**   this and *powder* (line 37) are favoured by Tina because they are associated with white people.

36–8 Lawino's feeling *sick* and laying *ghosts* highlights the culture clash between the two types of woman.

49 Tina's pallor as a result of using face powder sound unnatural and diseased once more, reinforced by *sickly* (line 50).

58–60 The exclamatory tone here shows Lawino to be almost incredulous, and presents Tina as foolish in her attempts to alter her identity.

80–81 How do you respond to these lines?

94 **the beautiful woman**   by now this phrase used to describe Tina carries a heavy weight of irony.

97–102   This description continues the tone of incredulity as Lawino's comparisons and analogies become increasingly personal and exaggerated.

106–9   Lawino's disingenuous description of Western underwear characterizes the bra as almost a weapon. The use of the metaphor of *nests* (begun in line 99) continues for so long and in such detail that it becomes a poetic conceit (a comparison that is sustained for some lines).

110–12   **the men believe/They are holding the waists/Of young girls** this implies deceit on the part of women like Tina, and gullibility on the part of men who are confused by the identity of such women.

115–16   Tina is depicted as a much older woman than she seems, disguising her true self to be more appealing.

117–18   As a result of suckling *many kids* she is no longer womanly, but the *nests* give her a false identity as a younger woman.

Digging: Seamus Heaney (1966)

Seamus Heaney was born in 1939 in Northern Ireland, and was the eldest of nine children in a farming family. This poem comes from his 1966 collection *Death of a Naturalist*. In it he examines his identity as a writer and looks at his struggle to come to terms with who and what he is. Coming from a humble farming background but having been university educated, Heaney is acutely aware of being educated 'out of his tribe'. In other words, he sees himself as separate from his family and his ancestors because he has had the benefit of learning and they have not.

Being part of a family is one way in which identity is defined and preserved. His father and grandfather before him were 'diggers', either in the soil or on the peat bog to cut the turf for fuel. Heaney, however, is a writer and thus does not share in the family identity.

The central dilemma of this poem is how to reconcile these two parts of his identity, as both a member of a farming family and a member of the literary fraternity. As he writes, his dilemma is solved simultaneously with the poem being written. Ultimately, he can use his pen as a tool, *Just like his old man* (line 16). Instead of a spade digging into the earth or into the peat bog, his pen will do the digging into his family's past. As the peat bog represents, in its various layers, the past of the land, so his head is a repository of his family's past. His central realization that with his pen he can recreate this past, and maintain the sense of the family's identity, resolves the problem of what his own identity is. He too is a digger, but with a pen, not a spade.

Notice Heaney's use of *under, down, bends, buried* and *down and down*, and his repetition of the poem's title word *digging*, all of which suggest delving into the earth and correspondingly into its and his family's past.

Notice also the sensuousness of the descriptions of the act of digging, and consider the synesthesia (blending of the senses) in *cold smell* and *the squelch and slap/Of soggy peat*. Look at the precision with which the tasks of digging are described, for example in lines 10–11. Why do you think Heaney does this?

1 The precision of the placing of the pen implies the care involved in writing. This precision is also apparent in his descriptions of his father's work with his spade.

2 **rests** this implies the writer's present inactivity, in contrast to his father's activity outside.
snug as a gun what is your response to this simile?

7 This line deftly shifts the time of the poem into the past.

15–16 These lines shift the poem further into the past to the poet's grandfather's time. *By God* implies admiration of their skill; *old man* is a reference to literal age but also implies a fond form of address. Both men have a clear identity as masters of their craft.

26 **the curt cuts** a combination of alliteration, assonance and consonance create an onomatopoeic effect so that we experience the sound and feel of the action of digging, just as the poet does.

27 **living roots awaken in my head** the literal roots in the earth have become the metaphorical roots of his family – its identity – which he carries in his brain.

28 The poet ruefully seeing himself as inferior. He cannot dig as his forefathers did and other men still do.

29–30 Repetition of the opening sentence at the end of the poem gives a sense of completion.

31 The addition of this line suggests a realization of the poet's identity and worth as a digger who can delve into and explore his family's past, recreating it on paper.

Follower: Seamus Heaney (1966)

One of several poems about family, *Follower* is, like *Digging* (see above) from the 1966 collection *Death of a Naturalist* and explores the idea of following on from the previous generation. It depicts the child's struggle to be like his father, a farmer who can plough with precision and skill, *An expert* while he as a child is *a nuisance*.

The verbs associated with the father – *set* (line 5), *fit* (line 6), *narrowed* and *angled* (line 11) – suggest precise actions completed successfully.

The present participles used to describe the boy – *Dipping and rising* (line 16), *tripping, falling/ Yapping* (lines 21–2) – imply actions which are incomplete or unproductive, suggesting his incompetence.

Ironically, once the struggle to emulate the expert father is achieved, in a cruel reversal, the father becomes the follower who *keeps stumbling*, and the two have effectively exchanged identities.

However, the last stanza can be interpreted in another way, and the claim in the final line that the father *will not go away* can be seen as an assertion of a family identity, a bond that cannot be broken between father and son.

2 **like a full sail strung** this simile depicts the father as ship-like with shoulders like a *sail*, and a *wake* (line 13) behind. The assonance and alliteration suggest roundness as well as fullness.

17 This line sums up the idea that the boy wants to resemble his father in adulthood, to carry on the tradition.

19 This line sums up what the narrator sees as his inadequacy. To be a follower is not the same as being the instigator, the doer.

The Early Purges: Seamus Heaney (1966)

Another poem from the collection *Death of a Naturalist* (see *Digging* and *Follower* above), this poem looks retrospectively at the loss of innocence of the narrator. He was a young boy when he *first saw kittens drown* and has over time come to see his supposedly *false sentiments* displaced by *living* (line 16). The use of *first* suggests a series of such events on farms, where he claims to feel as an adult that *pests have to be kept down.*

The struggle to come to terms with the violence of this rite of passage (first witnessing a death) takes the passage of time, reflected by the use of enjambement across not just lines but between stanzas 4 and 5. The poet's use of rhyme is effective in suggesting that time does not diminish sense impressions, in particular sounds.

In the title, the word *Early* could refer to the young age of the child or that of the kittens, or even to the time of day. *Purges* carries associations with cleansing, flushing out and emptying the bowels, all of which imply the removal of waste, which is how *Dan Taggart* regards the kittens: to him they are *scraggy wee shits* and they end up like *dung* (line 12).

1 **drown** the first line of the first stanza ends with this word and it becomes the chief rhyming sound at the beginning and end of the poem. This echoing runs through the poem, as *drown* is repeated in line 17. With the rhymes in lines 19 and 21, it is as if the noise still resounds in his head despite the passage of time, so that ultimately, despite appearances, he does not identify with the likes of *Dan Taggart* but with *sentiments.*

8 **Like wet gloves** this simile depicts how the child sees the dead kittens, as if maintaining the integrity of their shape.

9 **glossy and dead**   this oxymoronic (self-contradictory) detail is
 ironic since *glossy* implies health, the opposite of *dead*.

16 This line marks a change in tone and a shift to adulthood for
 the narrator, complemented by a shift to polysyllables. What is
 your response to the tone here?

18 **It makes sense**   this brief, terse and monosyllabic cliché puts a
 stop to speculation and places *sense* in opposition to *sentiments*.

21 What is your reading of the poem's final line?

The Joy of Writing: Wislawa Szymborska (1967)

Wislawa Szymborska was born in 1923 in Kornik, Poland and is
well regarded in her country as well as abroad. Her work reflects
on the human condition and the puzzles and paradoxes of our
existence. It has been translated into several languages, but her
output is small and she does not seek publicity. She was awarded
the Nobel Prize for Literature in 1966.

The Joy of Writing comes from her 1967 collection *Sto pociech*
(*No End of Fun*). In it she gives to the writer the ultimate power
of control over her creation. Whereas in Ted Hughes's poem *The
Thought-Fox* (see page 28) the poet's identity is subsumed by
poetic inspiration, Szymborska's creation – a doe – is totally
dependent for its identity on her. It might struggle, but in the end
the power lies in the poet's armoury of *letters up to no good* and
clutches of clauses. Their personification gives them power but in
the end they are *so subordinate* to the writer that she holds sway
over them, and thus over the doe, as *Not a thing will ever happen
unless I say so* (line 23).

The imagery throughout is of writing and printing.

1 Immediately, the repetition of *written* sets up the notion that
 the *doe* is a product of the poet. The question form of this first
 line invites readers into a kind of debate.

6 **beneath my fingertips**   it is clear that the doe is reliant for her
 identity on the poet.

14–17 **ink... hunters... guns** the imagery of ink and pen as weapons makes the identity of the doe even more precariously dependent on the whim of the writer.

20–21 The opposition between the extremes of a tiny moment (the *twinkling of an eye*) and infinite time (*eternities*) makes clear the unlimited power of the poet, against which there can be no struggle by the doe.

23 This line reinforces the notion of the poet as standing in the place of a creator god with unlimited power. This identity is secure and unquestionable, whereas that of the created being, the doe, is not.

30–32 These last three lines build up to a climax in which the poet is exultant about her own supremacy. There is no struggle here; the facts are presented as incontrovertible.

The French Lieutenant's Woman: John Fowles (1969)

John Fowles (1926–2005) was educated at Oxford, became a teacher, and worked for a time in Greece, which influenced the writing of his novel *The Magus* (1965). He is well known for his 1963 novel *The Collector*, which was made into a film featuring Terence Stamp. In 1968 he and his wife moved to Lyme Regis, which is where *The French Lieutenant's Woman* is set and where he died in November 2005.

The novel, published in 1969 but set in Victorian England and following the Victorian novelist's convention of using poems, extracts, proverbs and maxims in each chapter heading, is very clearly not Victorian. This is made evident by the way that the author's dialogue with the reader reaches proportions usually not seen in novels of the late nineteenth and early twentieth century.

Most notably, in Chapter 13 the authorial voice suspends the narrative of the lives of the main characters Charles and Sarah, leaving the latter at the end of Chapter 12 apparently teetering on her window sill, and asking us *Who is Sarah? Out of what shadows does she come?* His concern here, then, is apparently to examine the identity of his main female character while the narrative is left hanging.

At the same time, Fowles investigates the identity of the novelist, offering a variety of interpretations of his role and considering what the extent of his power or influence is with characters who effectively also have a will of their own.

His initial claim is that the characters are imaginary and exist in his mind only, but that he has to pretend to know and understand them. In this way the identity of the writer is one which *stands next to God* as a creator, but one who is not omniscient.

His other suggestions about the novelist include the idea that he is a kind of puppeteer, an autobiographer, a presence in his own text, and finally a creator of an alternative reality in which characters *begin to disobey* (line 59). As a result, ultimately there is a struggle between the creator (or god) of the characters and the characters he has created.

His idea is expanded when he writes of the character Charles gaining *autonomy* and the author having to allow him what are ultimately his own choices of action. He justifies this by saying that *to be free myself* he has to grant his characters their freedom too.

The novelist's identity, then, is in some ways subordinated to that of the characters, and, he adds, *I do not fully control these creatures* (lines 92–3).

His final point in this dialogue with his readers concerns us; we, he claims, have a fictionalized idea of our own identity, not considering our own past as real but altering it so that it becomes more fiction than fact.

His conclusion is that as far as a sense of our own identity goes, we are in flight from it or from *the real reality*, and that this is what it is to be human.

    1 **I do not know**   this follows on from the question at the end of the previous chapter. It is a brief and succinct way of signalling an abdication of the novelist's role as omniscient controller of the narrative. There is no struggle here. Fowles

simply shifts the perspective and presents himself as a pretender rather than a director.

12 **So perhaps** this signals the beginning of a series of alternative identities for the novelist – as a writer of autobiography, as an essayist, as a string-puller for puppets, as a person in his own novel. His detached tone throughout is interesting, as is the fact that this is presented as a dialogue with the reader. What is your response to this tone and to the idea of being directly addressed by the author?

41–4 **You may think... Chapter Thirteen** this continues the dialogue with us as readers. The use of the verb form *may* suggests that we could be wrong.

47 **skilled furniture-makers** what is your response to this analogy?

52–3 *we wish to create... that is* putting this claim in italics makes its importance clear. The idea of an alternative or parallel reality is fundamental to the nature of all fiction and suggests that the identity of the characters is and is not real.

58–60 **It is only... begin to live** this suggests that there is a struggle by the characters to achieve an autonomous identity.

61–2 **I ordered him... But he did not** this is a clear statement of Charles's autonomy, suggesting that the character has an identity of his own and that it is at odds with that of the creator.

68–9 **and I am the most reliable witness** Fowles's tone in this parenthetical phrase is ironic. Why do you think he uses this tone?

69–70 **the idea... Charles, not myself** this reinforces the idea that the character is autonomous; he has established an identity of his own that can override the will of his creator.

71 **I must respect it** the role of the creator is subordinate here.

74–9 **to be free... conform to that definition** these lines sum up Fowles's key idea that the novelist is like God in granting freedom, or free will, to those whom he has created, thus freeing himself. So the identity of the character and that of her/his author are mutually interdependent.

92–6 **I do not fully control... even yourself** by linking his position as author to that of the reader as a person who might wish to be in control, he is able to conclude that we are not in control. The argument suggests that we too do not have the autonomy we think we have, and that our identities are not as clearly fixed as we suppose.

99–103 **You do not think… your romanced autobiography**   in this statement directed at the reader, Fowles seems to suggest that we have a fictive sense, rather than a real one, of who or what we are, that our identity is reworked by us into a form that we feel is fitting, even if it is at odds with reality. He implies that rather than being a struggle, we all do this naturally, and become the authors of our own novels, which are non-factual or unreal versions of our own lives.

103 **We are all in flight from the real reality**   the use of tautology *real reality* stresses the idea that identity is not unalterable but dependent on our tendency to avoid reality. There is no struggle; this is just what human beings do.

103–4 **That is a basic definition of *Homo sapiens***   the use here of the Latin term for 'human being', plus the idea of *definition*, implies that we cannot help the way we are because fictionalizing ourselves and making up *romanced* identities is what we do.

I Know Why the Caged Bird Sings: Maya Angelou (1969)

Born in 1928 in St Louis as Marguerite Johnson, Maya Angelou is perhaps the most well-known black female writer in the US. She is presently Reynolds Professor of American Studies at Wake Forest University in North Carolina, a position she has held since 1981.

Her autobiographical work *I Know Why The Caged Bird Sings* is her most famous and was followed by five more volumes, the last of which, *A Song Flung up to Heaven*, was published in 2002.

She has also written six collections of poetry, the inaugural poem for President Bill Clinton, several prize-winning documentaries, a screenplay and a ten-part television series on African traditions in American life.

In this, the first volume of her autobiography, Maya Angelou recreates her childhood years during which she and her brother Bailey lived with her grandmother and uncle in Stamps, a small town in Arkansas.

Her grandmother owns a store in which Uncle Willie (her son and Maya's uncle) works. Maya explains that he was crippled as a result of being dropped at three years of age by a babysitter. The grandmother holds *no rancour* against the woman who caused his lameness, adding that nevertheless *She felt it necessary to explain over and over again to those who knew the story by heart that he wasn't 'born that way'*.

This suggests that in the grandmother's eyes his disability is not part of her son's original or real identity. How he deals with it on one particular day points up some interesting ideas about what does constitute a person's identity in their own and other people's eyes, and how it might not be a constant.

In the extract Uncle Willie, to his niece's astonishment, disguises his disability and succeeds in deceiving a pair of strangers who come into the store. He virtually assumes a new identity, and it is not without a struggle.

3–5 **Uncle Willie… and underpaid** this makes clear how he is perceived by those in the community who have little work or money.

6–7 **a double-tiered barrier in his path** this presents his problems as almost insurmountable.

7–10 **He was… by his defect** in a rational and balanced way, the narrator sums up the double bind he is in.

11–13 **Only once… lame** the fact that this statement stands alone as a one-sentence paragraph makes obvious the uniqueness of the event she is about to describe.

18 **I sensed a wrongness** at this stage the narrator intuitively feels that all is not right, but is not yet aware of the facts.

23–4 **When I looked… my mind's coattails** this creates suspense as we wait to discover what the narrator has discovered.

24–6 **He was standing erect… Erect** the repetition of *erect* suggests the narrator's incredulity.

27–8 **a mixture of threats and appeal**   the signal he is sending out is paradoxical and the identity he is projecting is unclear. He is presenting himself to the strangers as not lame, although he is; he is also the narrator's superior in age, but has put himself in her power.

30 **his walking stick… was nowhere to be seen**   a sure sign of the true physical state of Uncle Willie, the stick, is hidden, as is this part of his identity.

33 **th-th-these days**   Willie's stutter is represented, while at the same time he is depicted as playing the role of an adult experienced in the task of parenting, and complicit with the strangers in sharing knowledge about children.

48–9 **He tried a laugh**   Willie is becoming experimental in his attempt to perfect the illusion that is his new identity.

51 **I didn't mind his using us to make himself look good**   the narrator's tolerant understanding here shows her maturity.

59–66 **Uncle Willie was making his way… wooden support**   this description presents the reality of Uncle Willie's physical condition, which he has successfully hidden from the strangers. The fact that it has been a struggle is clear from the choice of present participles, which make his actions seem continuous and unfinished.

69 **a whole Mr Johnson**   the use of the formal name makes him indeed seem like the different person whose identity he has assumed.

71 **He must have tired of being crippled**   the narrator shows understanding. She writes here as if *being crippled* is an identity, which along with being the butt of the jokes of others is one a person can become exhausted by.

76–7 **for one afternoon… he wanted no part of them**   the space of time during which Uncle Willie took on the identity of *erect* Mr Johnson is narrowed precisely, the more to focus the reader's mind on how much time he spends struggling, *lurching* and *bumping* in his identity as the crippled Uncle Willie.

The Female Eunuch: Germaine Greer (1970)

Born in Australia in 1939, Germaine Greer took a scholarship at Cambridge University in 1964, gained a PhD in 1968 and accepted a lecturing post at Warwick University. She has had a distinguished academic career but is perhaps best known today for her television appearances and for *The Female Eunuch*.

When it was first published in 1970, this book caused such a stir that in some households it was allegedly thrown across rooms or over dinner tables. The idea of a eunuch who is female is central to the thesis of the text: that women are subjected to a process which is like the castration of animals, which leaves them – again like animals – weakened and easily manipulated by men.

Her main argument is that if women were to realize their potential and not only see themselves in traditional female roles as mothers, wives, sisters and daughters (always in relation to and subordinate to men), civilization would be life-centred rather than driven by the aggression, war and power struggles that are in general more typical of male rather than female behaviour.

This extract is from Chapter 3, 'Baby', of the second part, 'Soul'. In it she draws a comparison between the ways *little boys* and *little girls* are brought up. She argues that the way girls are conditioned – chiefly by their mothers – leads to them seeing themselves as, and in some ways becoming, victims. By the time they reach school, they are conditioned to be quiet and self-effacing, are channelled into domestic tasks and are looked upon with suspicion if they have intellectual leanings.

What is your response to the comparison between Virginia Woolf and George Eliot (both successful women novelists) which ends this extract?

1–2 **Little boys… encouraged to**   the triadic structure of this
    sentence suggests a logical developmental sequence for boys.

  2 **Little girls are not**   contrastingly brief, this sentence implies a
    lack of development.

4–5   **more relentlessly supervised and repressed**   this implies that the girl's identity is deliberately given little scope to develop, unlike a boy's.

9–10   **punishments… for wandering off on her own**   this suggests that female children's independence is disallowed.

10–11   **little boys are forming groups… she is isolated at home**   again this makes clear how the development of boys' identities is unhindered, but girls' are clearly circumscribed.

12–14   **Her comparative incarceration… the most dangerous place there is**   how do you respond to this statement?

15   **She is taught to fear and distrust the world at large**   this creates the sense that a girl's identity becomes linked with fear early in her development.

20–7   **When a little girl… strangled her**   how do you respond to this anecdote?

30–1   **frightened and guilty, as well as too worried**   the use of three adjectives here depicts girls as being dominated by negative emotions.

33–4   **think of themselves as victims**   here Greer implies that this is an identity in itself. Being a victim defines behaviour.

40–2   **little boys are learning… outside their homes**   in another triadic structure, a feature of her rhetoric, Greer links male identity with things external and involving other people.

42–3   **little girls are… helping Mother**   this list, somewhat longer than the previous one, implies retreat, being silenced and isolation. The phrase *or helping Mother* is set against all this, but is not presented as an attractive alternative, implying as it does that the girls conform to the mothers' mould.

44–6   **they use their energy… hearing and doing**   another list of three depicts girls as using their powers paradoxically to be self-effacing, denying any impulses such as those that typify boys, and thus their individual identity.

The Badness Within Him: Susan Hill (1973)

Susan Hill was born in Scarborough in 1942 and is a prolific writer of fiction for adults and children, as well as of non-fiction. Between 1968 and 1974 she produced eight titles, one of which is the short story collection *A Bit of Singing and Dancing*, from which *The Badness Within Him* comes. This collection deals with themes such as isolation and alienation, as well as lack of communication and frustration.

In *The Badness Within Him* the main character, Col, a young boy about to enter his teenage years, is convinced that there is *badness* inside him. He feels anger towards his family while on their annual holiday to a seaside resort. The phrase in the title is used frequently throughout the story and becomes almost a defining description of the identity against which he struggles.

In his frustration he hopes for change, *some terrible event, violence* and *an end to everything*, and is irritated by others' suggestions about what he might do. He is so angered and frustrated by the demands of his family that he leaves them and strides off alone to a cliff top, from where he can see his father swimming.

The story ends when something does happen that creates an irrevocable change: his father is drowned, a cathartic experience for Col, which he blames on his own *badness*.

1–2 **Now he felt rested... above it all**   away from his family at the top of the hill overlooking the sands, Col is literally and metaphorically *above it all* as he begins to consider himself and his situation in his struggle to understand himself.

7–8 **Col thought... badness within me**   this is one of several attempts Col makes in his struggle to rationalize his behaviour and to understand why he is so angry and frustrated. The phrase *the badness within me* becomes part of his identity, a part of which only he is aware.

24–6 **we will never be the same... separate people now**   this marks an epiphanic moment for Col as he becomes aware that as from this moment things have changed, which is what he wanted originally. He is also aware of his identity as separate from the rest of his family.

30 **Col saw that his father was drowning** this is presented matter-of-factly, without emotion. The fact that it is a one-sentence paragraph gives it prominence and power. The break in the narrative suggests that Col does not react to what he sees for some time.

33–4 **Col looked at the cliff, falling away at his feet** this, his first reaction to his father's drowning, suggests that he is literally and metaphorically on the edge of an abyss as he struggles to come to terms with what has happened.

34–6 **He closed his eyes… his hands and knees** this intensifies the idea of the struggle, both literal and metaphorical.

37 **His head was hot and throbbing** Col's crisis reaches a climax.

39–40 **his father's body… and shivered** the use of the clinical word *body* makes clear that his father has indeed drowned. Col's shivering is juxtaposed with this, suggesting that his coldness is the result not just of being in the shadow of the cliff but also being close to his father's corpse.

57–61 **In bed… I am punished** Col's reaction implies his feelings of guilt over his father's death. His feeling of responsibility for that part of himself which *made it come about* leads as if logically to the idea of paying for a crime.

68–9 **He stared, trying to feel some sense of loss and sorrow** Col struggles to react emotionally to the sight of his father's corpse.

72 **understood better** this implies that Col is coming to a realization of what really happened, and that he didn't cause his father's death.

76–7 **Then, he knew that the change had come** this creates an air of finality. This is what Col had been struggling towards, though not in this way.

77–9 **knew that the long, hot summer… house again** these words complete a lengthy sentence, which suggests the long period of the struggle Col has undergone.

79–80 **He knew, finally, the power of the badness within him** this reiterates the idea of there being a hidden part to Col, which now has a kind of supremacy as part of his identity.

81–2 **he wept** how do you respond to these last two words?

This Be The Verse: Philip Larkin (1974)

Philip Larkin (1922–1985) was a poet and novelist who spent his working life as a university librarian. This is one of the briefer poems from Larkin's collection *High Windows*. It is typical of Larkin in that the apparent casualness of the language, including as it does taboo words, is framed by a strict stanzaic form and a disciplined rhyme scheme.

The main idea of the poem – that parents unwittingly ruin their children's lives, having previously been *fucked up in their turn*, contrasts with other texts (for example *Mr Pip*, see page 83) where the passing on of family characteristics is celebrated.

The title of *This Be The Verse* is a humorous parody of religious language (see Interpretations page 164), and sets the tone for the poem.

1 **fuck you up**   the language might shock, but it can be taken as a pun: they wreck your life/ they give you life. The second-person address is unusual and draws in the reader, in contrast to the possibly repelling effect of the use of non-poetic diction.
   mum and dad   this sounds cosily colloquial, again at odds with the taboo words.
6 **fools**   used to describe the previous generation, this carries on the idea of damage being unwitting rather than intentional.
7 **soppy-stern**   this neatly oxymoronic term implies a sense of confusion about discipline and feelings.
9 This line has the ring of religious language and echoes the tone of the title.
10 **like a coastal shelf**   how do you respond to this image?

Woman Work: Maya Angelou (1978)

For brief information about Maya Angelou, see page 111. The poem *Woman Work* comes from her 1978 collection *And Still I Rise*. The narrator's struggle to find time for herself is overshadowed by the almost endless list of tasks she has to perform for others. She is almost defined by the work she has to do for *children*, *company* and *the sick*. All that she has for herself are the natural elements such as *sunshine* and *rain*, which might bring her respite.

The form of the poem is interesting. The second part, beginning *Shine on me*, is presented in a series of neatly structured four-line stanzas, using simple rhymes which impose a sense of order after the first stanza's almost random selection of jobs to be done.

1–14   The fact that this first stanza is presented as one long list complements the idea that the number of tasks the woman has to perform is almost endless. It is as if once one job is done another inexorably follows. The colloquial variations on the form 'I have to' – *I've got, I got, I gotta* – reinforce the idea of necessity, of being compelled to do the 14 tasks listed.

15–18   The personification of sunshine and rain here, and later other elemental forces, gives them power to counterbalance the weight of the previous long stanza. What is your response to the tone here?

19–22   This is perhaps the narrator's strongest assertion. The idea of floating *across the sky* suggests that perhaps she can only be herself if she is all but obliterated.

23–4   **snowflakes/Cover me**   this reinforces this idea of gaining one's sense of self only when obliterated.

27–30   This stanza supports the idea that it is only when among the elements that the woman's work is made secondary. Whereas her work has owned her, she suggests that the elements, by contrast, are hers and that because she can call them her own, they define her ultimately as she becomes part of the natural world.

The Company of Wolves: Angela Carter (1979)

Angela Carter (1940–1992) was a novelist whose interests included feminism and traditional story-telling. This short story is part of the werewolf trilogy at the end of the collection *The Bloody Chamber*. The story itself is made up of four tales and the extract comes from the last of these four.

In the seventeenth century, Charles Perrault wrote 'Little Red Riding Hood' and other stories with the purpose of warning readers, especially girls and young women, about the sexual threat embodied in men (see the headnote to Carol Ann Duffy's *Little Red-Cap*, page 142).

Angela Carter, with a modern feminist agenda and a desire to subvert the original genre, produced stories – especially the werewolf trilogy – which put a new twist on Perrault's tales and moral purposes. Instead of showing vulnerable females needing to be warned about or protected from males, her stories depict female characters as strong and able to prevail over men, even when they take the identity of the wolf. The concept of the werewolf is crucial, as it implies the ability to shift identity from man to wolf and back again. Similarly we see a shift in identity for the unnamed heroine, from potential victim, to *nobody's meat*, to willing partner of the wolf.

In this extract, the young man, who has met and talked with the girl in the forest, has made a bet with her that he will reach her grandmother's house before she does. When he asks what she will give him if he arrives first, she asks him *What would you like?* The fact that she does this *disingenuously* suggests that she enters a sort of game with him and does so knowingly. His reply is *A kiss*, which when they meet inside her grandmother's house she gives *freely*. The girl acknowledges her debt and keeps to the bargain without being forced to. She is clearly her own person.

The young man impersonates the girl, taking on her identity, to insinuate himself into the grandmother's house, but his encounter with the older woman is sexual rather than simply murderous.

When the girl arrives he reverses the process and takes on the identity of the grandmother. Once she is alone with the young man she is quite aware of the danger she is in. Instead of being frightened she realizes that *fear did her no good* so *she ceased to be afraid* (line 29). She proves to be the wolf's equal, even laughing at him, and maintains her sense of self.

The story ends with the unnamed heroine safe but choosing to be with the man who is also the wolf.

1–2 **Where is... my darling** while this question emphasizes the girl's vulnerability, the statement by the young man in reply is suggestive of a loving encounter.

4–5 **the howling of a multitude of wolves** this intensifies the sense of danger.

5–6 **she knew the worst wolves are hairy on the inside** this is a reference to the werewolf myth and the idea that, according to Perrault, 'all wolves are not of the same sort'.

6–9 **the scarlet shawl... red as the blood she must spill** this is at once a reminder of the red of the original riding hood and an ambiguous allusion to her killing of the man/wolf or losing her virginity.

11–12 **I love the company of wolves** notice the use of the story's title. It might suggest that the young man is a werewolf, but also presents wolves as literally companionable. The identity of the man/wolf, the girl and the wolves all shift from their norms.

19 **howling as if their hearts would break** this phrase is anthropomorphic (describes the animals as if they have human characteristics), and makes the wolves seem worthy of the pity she extends to them.

26 **threnody** a song of lamentation.

27–8 **her scarlet shawl... the colour of her menses** how do you respond to the rich symbolism here?

45–6 **went directly to the man** this makes it clear that the girl does not retain the identity of a victim as in the original story. She is willing to share the man's bed.

49–50 **What big arms... hug you with** this is a parody of the original fairy tale, and suggestive of a loving embrace.

51 **prothalamion** a song or poem in celebration of marriage. This detail sees the wolves as a kind of congregation at a wedding ceremony.

52–3 **she freely gave the kiss she owed him** she seals her bargain made with the young man in the forest, now the man/wolf in the bed.

56 **Liebestod** erotic death or love death; two lovers' consummation of their love in death establishes the wolf/man and girl/woman as lovers. The imminence of her destruction is clarified by the next line.

59 **All the better to eat you with** this echoes the original story. Here, however, the nameless heroine's laughter changes the mood.

60–1 **she knew she was nobody's meat** she has total confidence in a self that is not victim but partner.

64 **Walpurgisnacht** the night of the witches' sabbath, implying magical transformations.

67 **Carnivore incarnate** this phrase has an almost religious ring to it. *Incarnate* means 'made flesh'. Christ was God incarnate; correspondingly, the wolf (*carnivore*, flesh-eater) is made man in a *Walpurgisnacht* shift of identity.

68–71 **She will lay… marriage ceremony** how do you respond to this sentence?

79–80 **Christmas Day, the werewolves' birthday** this continues the theme of magic and paganism.

82 **sweet and sound** this echoes the reassuring cliché 'safe and sound', but adds 'sweetness'.

82–3 **in granny's bed, between the paws of the tender wolf** the unnamed heroine is secure. The juxtaposition of *granny's bed* and the wolf's *paws* is arresting and indicates an identity gained in part from her past (her grandmother) and from her chosen future (with the wolf). This last detail is reminiscent of Carol Ann Duffy's poem *Little Red-Cap*, where she slides between the wolf's *heavy matted paws* (see page 76).

Nella Last's War: eds Richard Broad and Suzie Fleming (1981)

Nella Last, an ordinary housewife, was asked in 1939 by the Mass Observation Archive, a government social research organization, to keep a regular diary. The text from which this comes is just a section of what became the work of 30 years. Part of it was recently the subject of the television film *Housewife, 49*.

Here Nella is describing events during the Second World War when the daughter of one of the group of voluntary workers to which she belongs has a baby. This rite of passage, the addition of a child to the family, is not greeted with joy, however. The mother has been unable to marry the father because he has been posted abroad. The consequences are tragic.

The extract focuses on family relationships and the struggle to keep a sense of family bonds in times of war. The family members are all unnamed, and the fact that we do not know their identities universalizes their circumstances. What happens to them could happen to anyone. Referring to the people involved in terms of their relationship with one another creates a sense of closeness. The *adored daughter* becomes *the mother*, which makes clear the shift in identity that the birth of the child has occasioned; tragically, the young woman abandons the struggle to occupy this identity.

1 **One of our members**   tactfully, Nella does not reveal names in her account.

  trouble   a term often used euphemistically to describe unhappy events in family circles, such as a death. Here, ironically, it is being used to refer to the opposite, the start of life for a child and the move into motherhood for an unnamed young woman.

  adored   this emphasizes the love felt by the mother for her daughter.

2 **young soldier father**   this phrase locates his identity as a member of the forces first, as a father second. It is as if being a soldier is a defining characteristic displacing his identity as a father. It does, in fact, define the nature of the family's

struggle to be a family, as his posting abroad has brought about the crisis.

4–5 **the daughter went to stay with an aunt**   again the family bonding is clear, but also the sense of *'disgrace'* (line 10). Unmarried women with babies often went away to hide what was perceived as their shame. The daughter's struggle against being identified as an unmarried mother in her own locality means she has to hide in *the Lakes*.

5–6 **We never mentioned it**   this makes clear again the tact of the others and their wish not to cause further pain.

10 **'disgrace'**   the inverted commas indicate that although society might see the illegitimate birth as shameful, Nella and her friends do not.

11–12 **such a wistful-eyed, solemn mite**   the detail about the baby makes clear its appeal and vulnerability to Nella and her friends. This is juxtaposed with the description of the ailing mother; the baby's very existence is the cause of her troubles.

12 **no hope at all for the mother's recovery**   this is a euphemistic way of indicating that she will die. She has given up the struggle to be a mother.

13 **From apathy and fretting, she has drifted into T.B.**   the list implies a steady decline from one stage to another. *T.B.* is tuberculosis, a condition that was frequently fatal at this time.

14–15 **She has no interest in her baby**   this is a denial of family bonding and the life-giving process. The baby's mother seems to be struggling against being a parent.

15–16 **its father's frantic loving letters**   the young man involved is now more obviously identified by his paternal relationship with the child rather than as a soldier. His struggle is *frantic*, implying his desperation to comfort his partner and to be acknowledged as father to her child.

17–18 **she cannot bear him hatred for the 'ruin of her daughter's life'**   the young woman's mother cannot hate the father of the child, even though her own child's life has been ruined. The use of pronouns instead of names may cause difficulty, but ensures confidentiality. The word *ruin* was often used as a euphemism for the situation where a woman bears a child outside marriage. Here the meaning is also that the life of the daughter is about to end.

19 **Just another of Hitler's crimes**   Nella blames the war, and in
particular Adolf Hitler, the leader of the Third Reich with
which Britain was at war, for the separation which has caused
these sad circumstances.

19–20 **There was so little we could say and nothing we could do**
this balanced and almost antithetical sentence sums up Nella's
philosophical response to the situation. Clearly she and the
others feel powerless.

The Color Purple: Alice Walker (1982)

First published in 1982 and awarded the Pulitzer Prize for Fiction
in 1983, *The Color Purple* is one of numerous novels, non-fiction
works, and short story and poetry collections by Alice Walker.
She was born in 1944, is a firm campaigner for black and
women's rights, and was married for eight years to a Jewish civil
rights lawyer, Mel Leventhal. This inter-racial marriage brought
her threats from the Ku Klux Klan.

The Color Purple is perhaps her best-known work. It received
criticism from those who thought it depicted African-American
men as abusive or foolish.

The main character, Celie, is the chief narrative voice in a
series of letters to God (and to her absent sister). Celie's style and
vocabulary develops as she does, from *poor, black and ugly* to an
assertive and confident woman with her own business. She
achieves this mainly through the love of Shug Avery, a beautiful
singer and lover of Celie's husband, whom she calls only
Mr_____. His full identity is never revealed, though at times
he is referred to as *Albert* by Shug.

Earlier, Celie has described Sofia as the sort of woman who
don't even deal in little ladyish things such as slaps, because when
slapped by Squeak, her husband's new mistress, she retaliates so
violently that she *knock two of Squeak's side teef out*. Thus her self-
assertiveness is established before we hear the story of how she
comes to be in jail. In the extract, Celie is telling Squeak that Sofia

has just been arrested and is now imprisoned for *Sassing the* (white) *mayor's wife*. In fact, she has been so severely beaten that she loses the sight of one eye.

The issue at stake for Sofia is her identity as a free black woman of some substance. She has been patronized by the mayor's wife, who asks her to become her maid, which is reminiscent of the master/slave relationship that characterized an earlier era in America. It is a principle for which Sofia is willing to fight, literally, and for which she will sacrifice her freedom.

4 **Sassing the mayor's wife**   to be 'sassy' is, in colloquial American English, to be impertinent or insolent. It is a variant of being 'cheeky'.

7 **Make Harpo call you by your real name**   Celie's advice to Squeak, that she should ask to be called by her *real name*, shows her awareness that names create one's identity, and diminutive ones like *Squeak* don't help.

11 **the prizefighter**   the man Sofia went off with after the fight with Squeak.

12–13 **Clam out on the street looking like somebody**   at this stage in the text Celie's language is more colloquial than it is in the closing stages. The reference to looking *like somebody* means that they look important or stylish.

15 **All these children**   there is an implied criticism of Sofia for having so many.

15–16 **digging in her pocketbook**   this might mean that she is about to give them money, which in Sofia's eyes would be insulting because it suggests that she cannot afford to care for the children.

17 **put her hand on one of the children head**   the gesture is a condescending one that might be used with a pet.

18 **and such strong white teef**   such a physical appraisal is more appropriate for a horse or other animal. The mayor's wife is not interested in their individual identities.

19–20 **Wait for her to pass**   their passivity is, we imagine, born out of patience and strength rather than subservience.

21 **watch her with a little smile**   the mayor seems to support his wife at this moment.

21–2 **Always going on over colored** the idea that she frequently wants to 'pet' black children – and perhaps adults – is suggested.

22–3 **Miss Millie finger the children some more** the juxtaposition of *Miss Millie* and *the children* gives her the status of a name and *the children* none, not even any individuality. The verb *finger* has unpleasant connotations, as if they were commodities.

23–4 **She look at the prizefighter car. She eye Sofia wristwatch** is Miss Millie sizing them up? Is she jealous? Is she incredulous that they appear to be so comfortably off?

25–6 **All your children so clean... be my maid?** the implication here is that Miss Millie is surprised as she expects black children to be dirty and their mother to be poor and needy. Her offer is either disingenuous or provocative.

27 **Hell no** Sofia's spontaneous reaction shows that she needs no such patronage. When she repeats it, it is for emphasis to assert herself as a person in her own right. When she says it the third time it is to outface the mayor, who demeaningly addresses her as *Girl* in public and in front of her children, as if she is a servant or even a slave.

33 **He slap her** this is on a line of its own to stress that it is an insult as well as an assault. Because he is mayor and white, and she a citizen and black, he feels that he can do this.

34 **I stop telling it right there** this is also on a line alone. Celie is tense because everyone knows what happens when Sofia is slapped.

40 **Sofia knock the man down** this reminds everyone of Sofia's fighting skills and her determination not to let anyone get the better of her.

41 **When I see Sofia I don't know why she still alive** this statement and the details which follow show how determined Sofia is to retain a sense of dignity and pride, to the extent that she nearly sacrifices her life as well as her freedom.

48–50 **I put it... and I start to work on her** Celie's tenderness is shown. Her practicality and care begin the process of restoring Sofia to the status of a person, not a victim, to help her regain her sense of identity.

I Coming Back: Grace Nichols (1983)

Born in Guyana in 1950, Grace Nichols's first years were spent in a coastal village. When she was eight her family moved to the city and her first novel, *Whole of a Morning Sky*, set in the middle of the country's struggle for independence, makes use of this experience.

Her years spent as a teacher and journalist as well as living in some very remote areas of Guyana were influential on her writing. Since 1977 she has lived in England and has written poems that reflect her influences.

Speaking about the language of her poetry, Nichols says that she likes to work in both Standard English and Creole, wanting to fuse the two because in her own background the two worlds were constantly interacting.

Some of her poems contain a flavour of the supernatural, and in *I Coming Back* we hear the distinctive voice of the female slave warning the slave master that she will return to haunt him after her death, in revenge for his treatment of her in life. It is a powerful assertion of her identity, one that will in the end overpower his.

1 **I coming back**   Nichols uses Creole to create the authentic voice of the slave-woman. The sentence is repeated at the end of each stanza, and is also the title. Its doubling at the start and end gives the poem an intensity like that of an incantation. The repetition of *I* shows her certainty about the new identity she will occupy.
   Massa   Master; the word is capitalized to give the effect that this is the slave owner's identity. He is simply to her a master, implying that she is the servant.

3 This title cleverly indicates that in the next world it is she who will be in charge: *mistress* is the counterpart to 'master'. The term *underworld* has connotations of otherness, of darkness and of spells, which is what the poem is, in effect. This is a powerful assertion of her identity.

6 **all that is evil**   this makes clear that when she returns it will be to do harm.

8–9 The revenge figure is brought uncomfortably close and is deceptively normal in form.

12 **skinless higue**   a vampiric figure in Caribbean folklore, a contrast to the familiarity of the dog.

14–15 An assault on the senses is suggested. The threat is becoming internalized.

17–18 Physical damage is implied, bringing the threat closer still.

21 This final (eleventh) statement has the effect of a prophesy. The emphatic use of *I* demonstrates that she will not be controlled and crushed in the future. It sees her in the role or identity of the *mistress*, the one who exerts the power.

The Handmaid's Tale: Margaret Atwood (1985)

Margaret Atwood, born in 1939 in Ottawa, is Canada's most celebrated and eminent writer, poet and critic and has won several literary awards as well as being presented with 12 honorary degrees. *The Handmaid's Tale* is set in the future republic of Gilead, in a dystopian society (one in which conditions are extremely bad; the opposite of a utopia). The novel received the Arthur C. Clark award for science fiction.

The narrator is called Offred; this is not her real name, but the name imposed on her because she is 'handmaid' to a man called Fred, and hence 'of' him. She narrates the tale of her previous and present life in a diary-like form, addressing unknown readers. Her life is circumscribed by the strict rules of the religious dictatorship that has taken over the country. For women, this means being assigned to one of a series of colour-coded identity groups, the chief of which are the Wives (blue), the Marthas (green), and the Handmaids – the bearers of the next generation – whose colour is red, symbolic of blood, fertility, and ironically the idea of the 'scarlet woman'.

In Chapter 22 Offred narrates from 'The Time Before' the revolution, describing the events of the day on which her identity – as a wife and mother with a career and a healthy bank balance, all of which were taken for granted – was removed from her.

In this extract, Offred describes the beginning of the assault on her identity, which is achieved by the simple method of erasing her bank account and dismissing her from her job, leading to the climax of the episode, when armed and uniformed men are seen in the corridor of the library where she works.

When she discovers that all accounts with the prefix 'F' are frozen, leaving only 'M' accounts active, it is clear that women *can't hold property any more... It's a new law*. This detail has echoes of nineteenth-century England, when all that a woman owned was by law passed to her husband on marriage. Women were virtually possessions of first their fathers and then their husbands, rather like Nora in *A Doll's House*.

The form of this extract is interesting: it consists of a series of short paragraphs interspersed with brief lines of dialogue, suggesting the speed at which events take place.

1 **It was after we'd been married, for year it seems**   this establishes a feeling of normality. It implies a routine, unremarkable existence; marriage is taken for granted.

1–2 **she was three or four**   this suggests the haziness of recollection.

3 **the usual way**   the emphasis is on the fact that everything was taken for granted.

12 **disappearances**   coming as it does at the end of a paragraph, the word presents the reader with a surprise. A note of discord is struck by the linking of this worrying word with children.

13–14 **the usual woman wasn't there**   this is a reverse echo of *the usual way* in line 3, signalling the beginning of a series of changes in her world.

14 **Instead there was a man, a young man**   this seems at first an innocuous detail, but the repetition of *man* fixes the change in the reader's mind. How do you respond to the short dialogue that follows?

30 **This number's not valid**   the chipping away of the narrator's security has begun. The repetition in the following lines of

number linked with *not valid* and *the red light* suggests that a brick wall of indifference from the young man and incomprehension from the narrator has to be negotiated.

31–2 **I've got thousands... two days ago**   these are markers of her identity – money brings security and independence.

53 **The lines were overloaded**   how do you respond to this?

56 **no luck**   this seems offhand; the narrator is philosophical.

57 **wasn't too unusual**   this is a change from *usual*, to suggest a shift in perception.

67 **let you go**   a euphemism for being sacked or fired.

89 **two men... in uniforms, with machine guns**   this indicates the deadly seriousness of the female workers' position. The appearance of these men in the corridor of the narrator's workplace ensures that she and her colleagues will co-operate in what is in fact the eradication of their individuality.

Beloved: Toni Morrison (1987)

Born in 1931 as Chloe Anthony Wofford, Toni Morrison changed her first name because classmates had difficulty pronouncing 'Chloe'. Interestingly, this extract from *Beloved* concerns names and their significance. However this is in the context of slavery, not a classroom.

Morrison's work has included teaching English at Howard University, working as an editor for Random House (where she specialized in black fiction), and more recently teaching creative writing at Princeton University. She is the first African-American woman to receive the Nobel Prize for Literature and has written several novels, of which *Beloved* is the most famous.

Set in 1873, the novel centres on the black slave experience, the power of memory and history. It treads the line between fact and fiction as some events are based on real experiences. The main character, Sethe, murders her youngest child to prevent her from having to live the life of a slave; this has echoes of the experience of Margaret Garner, who like Sethe escaped from slavery, murdered her child for a similar reason and was recaptured.

One of Morrison's aims in the text is to give a voice to those who have been denied one in the past and to recover a history lost to silence or deliberate forgetfulness. She writes the story of Sethe in a variety of voices, one of which is that of Sethe's mother-in-law, Baby Suggs.

The extract is from part of the text which focuses on Baby Suggs, who has been enslaved to Mr Garner and whose son Halle has worked to buy her freedom. She is now about to take a position as a liberated woman with the Bodwins.

In this extract, Baby Suggs is leaving the Garners' house on the way to the Bodwins and for the first time feels able to question her ex-slavemaster on the subject of her name.

By the time thy arrive at the Bodwins' house, her sense of self is clarified so that she introduces herself as 'Suggs', reinforcing it with the clarification 'Baby Suggs', and is addressed as 'Mrs Suggs' in return. This transformation from a sales-ticket name – 'Jenny' – and 'Whitlow', the name of her original owner, attests in part to Baby Suggs beginning to gain an identity of her own.

The form of the extract is mostly dialogue.

 2 **your sales ticket**   this makes clear that being a slave all but submerged Baby Suggs's identity. The fact that she was first identified by a price tag suggests that she is a commodity rather than a person.

2–3 **Ain't that... call yourself**   Morrison's use of colloquial language and ellipsis (missing out words) gives the flavour of American and Black American English of the time.

 4 **Nothing... I don't call myself nothing**   her reply emphasizes the point, as if naming herself is not her right.

 8 **sir**   notice how Baby Suggs addresses Mr Garner. Modes of address are of interest here for, although she is now a free woman, Mr Garner is referred to as a superior. She is *Jenny* (not her real name), *gal* or simply *you*.

10 **Anything**   her identity was not owned by herself, but by others, in particular her slavemasters. She has had no say in how she is addressed.

Suggs is what my husband name   this gives the flavour of Baby Suggs's speech and adds a layer of complexity. In her struggle to explain who she is not (*Jenny Whitlow*, her slave name) she takes the name of her 'husband', a married name of sorts, not a name of her own. At the time the text was written this would not have been unusual.

12 **Manner of speaking** this comment makes clear that the marriage was not a legal one (again not uncommon for slaves at the time). But her relationship to him is what she feels defines her as well as him.

22 **Baby** this also is a name her 'husband' called her, and so 'Baby Suggs' she is; but this first name too is not a name that truly identifies her, even though it is not a slave name.

24–5 **Mrs Baby Suggs ain't no name for a freed Negro** Garner's view is that this is at variance with her new liberated status. However, her identity is shown to be bound up with this name when we read the interior monologue that follows.

26–7 **all she had left** this poignant detail underlines the precariousness of the slave's existence, and reasserts the importance of names and naming in the struggle to gain a sense of self.

27 **'husband'** the inverted commas lay doubt on his identity.

59–70 How do you respond to the way in which introductions are made at the Bodwin house?

70 **I'm free, you know** this simple monosyllabic statement, in Standard English, makes clear Baby Suggs's status. Interestingly it comes second to establishing her name.

Making History: Brian Friel (1988)

Brian Friel, born in 1929 in Omagh, County Tyrone, is one of the foremost playwrights in Northern Ireland today. He began teaching in 1950 and had his first (radio) play produced on the BBC in 1958. He retired from teaching in 1960 and has written numerous plays, of which *Translations* and *Making History* are perhaps the most well known. He has also written short stories.

He helped to form the Field Day Theatre Company in 1980, which is committed to searching for the 'middle ground between the country's entrenched positions' (between the Catholic minority and the Protestant majority), in an attempt to help the Irish to explore new identities.

Friel's father was a teacher and his grandparents were illiterate agricultural workers whose first language was Irish. This has contributed to his interest in identity, which is a key theme in his work, along with ideas on truth and communication.

Identity, in Friel's view, is created through memory, and the collective memories of a community distinguish it from others. However, an individual's notion of what has occurred and what has formed him or her might be at odds with those of the community or those of another individual. Hence the question arises of whether it is possible to have a precise idea of a person's identity, given that even within the individual, there can be conflicting notions of who or what one is.

These ideas are central to *Making History*, which is set at the end of the sixteenth century. In this extract O'Neill, the play's main character, is at odds with Lombard, his biographer, about how he is being represented in Lombard's history. Also at issue is how O'Neill's wife Mabel will be represented, or indeed whether she will be included at all. O'Neill finds himself fighting for his own, albeit paradoxical, version of the 'truth' about himself, and against the merging of Mabel's identity with those of his other wives, to the point of near erasure.

O'Neill, now near the end of his life, has been a champion for his countrymen against the English in the time of Elizabeth I, and is now living in exile in Rome, with his last wife Catriona and his secretary Harry. He has little money, and is frequently – as here – the worse for drink.

4–5 **what we must remember… is the *whole* life**   Lombard is almost appropriating O'Neill's identity for the purposes of what he is recording.

8–9 **O'Neill was a household name right across Europe**   this is at odds with the situation O'Neill is in at present, giving rise to the question of who is the true O'Neill. The fact that he refers to his friend in the third person is interesting and suggests that

Lombard is seeing Hugh O'Neill as a name, as much as if not more than as a person. Names and their importance are key ideas in this passage and in Friel's work generally.

10–11 **not only by us but by the generations that follow us** this makes O'Neill the property of posterity, as if his identity is once again being appropriated by Lombard for the benefit of others.

14–17 **Mabel will be in the history, Peter?... Central to it, Peter** O'Neill makes clear that Mabel is fundamental to his notion of himself and that her identity is not to be overlooked or sidelined. Again, the use of names stands out as a further indicator of identity.

18–22 **And so will your first wife... all be mentioned** here Lombard makes clear that Mabel's identity, as only one of four wives, will be what he will establish. She is not to be identified as in any way special.

25–6 **there were rumours of a fifth** this makes Mabel seem even less important as an individual. Her identity is being submerged as part of a collective identity of wives in general.

34 **This is my last battle** in the past O'Neill has lost the battle of Kinsale (against English rule) and been humiliated by the Spanish and English. Now the motif of the battle becomes a way of characterizing the fight he is experiencing to be represented (and to have Mabel represented) to posterity in the way he regards as fitting and true.

40 *Your* **history** the emphatic *Your* stresses the idea that what is to be written is Lombard's version of the truth, and Lombard's version of O'Neill.

40–1 **I'm an old man... no money** this gives O'Neill's perception of himself, in contrast to Lombard's version of who he is or was.

41–3 **I'm not whingeing... going to win** paradoxically, though his fighting days are over, O'Neill still sees himself in the role of a man doing battle, though in a different way from that of the past.

61–4 **The schemer... put it *all* in** the list here indicates the multiplicity of identities O'Neill sees for himself. The pairings of near opposites, in terms of having a good or bad reputation (*schemer/leader*, *liar/statesman*, for example), indicate the paradox that is O'Neill's identity as well as the fact that there is, to him, more than a single self.

64 **Record the *whole* life**   in his view, he exists as the sum of these parts, paradoxical though the elements might be.

66 **Listen to me, Hugh**   cutting off Lombard here shows that O'Neill is taking the idea of the battle seriously.

68 **Don't embalm me**   O'Neill's identity is one that cannot be preserved and fixed. His view of himself is that his identity is composed of shifting extremes.

70–3 **That place is central to me… make Mabel central?**   the argument returns to where it began, with the idea of Mabel's fundamental importance to O'Neill shown by the repetition of *central*. She is not, in his mind, one of four or even five wives; she is an individual in her own right, and O'Neill battles to assert that identity for her.

An *Evil Cradling*: Brian Keenan (1992)

Born in Belfast in 1950, Brian Keenan took a degree in English Literature at Coleraine University, worked for a while in Brussels and in Spain, and returned to Ireland to teach and then to work in community development. After taking an MA in Anglo-Irish literature he went to Beirut in Lebanon to take up a post at the American University there.

In 1986, a year after his arrival, he was kidnapped by a Shi'ite fundamentalist group and held hostage for four and a half years. For some of the time that he was kept prisoner he shared a cell with John McCarthy, a journalist who ironically had originally come to Beirut to report on Keenan's plight.

In this extract from the chapter entitled 'Rape', first McCarthy and then Keenan have just experienced a prolonged and brutal beating from one of their captors, Said. Keenan feels that the *abuse of* his *body* was *a kind of rape* in which Said was the *violent lover* who was *sexually excited by what he was doing*.

Keenan's reaction is interesting and complex. He experiences not fear but a furious anger, which threatens to consume him so much that it *was greater than me*. It is as if his identity is subsumed by his fury. He also realizes, however, that his anger gives him strength and that part of his identity could never be taken away because *there was a sense of self greater than me*. By the end of the episode Keenan feels energized and refreshed and his sense of humour *came flowing back*, as if this too constitutes part of who and what he is.

2 **The smell of him, his sweet sickly perfume** this characterizes Said in terms of the sense of smell. It is as if this is the only power he has. Interestingly, *sweet* and *perfume* characterize him in a feminine rather than a masculine way, a subtle method of undermining his power.

4–6 **I wanted him to leave... this man had violated me** this crystallizes Keenan's reaction. He is not frightened by Said but the use of *violated* links with the concept of rape. Given that the majority of rape victims are women, it becomes essential to reassert his sense of masculine identity.

10–11 **a volcano in my chest... a subdued fury** the elemental image of the volcano suggests an anger that might explode, while his trembling is not from weakness but rage.

12–14 **an elemental anger... maintaining for myself** the suggestion here is interesting and complex: the anger is separate from Keenan's identity, which it is in a way suppressing, and he has another identity he has kept up for his own purposes which is also separate from the fury he feels.

14 **This was a rage that was greater than me** this implies that who or what Keenan is in that moment is subordinated to the rage he feels. The feeling seems to have an identity of its own which is stronger than his.

51–2 **The more I was beaten the stronger I seemed to become** this balanced and antithetical statement sums up the paradox that being the victim of abuse means a growth, not a diminution, in strength.

53–5 **a huge determination never... in front of them** the rhetorical triple *never* shows the strength of his determination to avoid giving in to his captors.

56–7 **not allow myself... I would humiliate them** again the rhetorical use of repetition lends power to his assertion of self.

58–9 **There was a part... take from me**   again the triple negative is powerful in clarifying the idea that one's identity remains intact and cannot be removed despite physical force.

59–60 **There was a sense of self greater than me alone**   this suggests that Keenan could not lose his identity because it was more than just himself. It exists as a part of himself, but also apart from himself.

Introduction to *Six Women Poets*: Grace Nichols (1992)

See page 128 above for brief information about Grace Nichols. In this introduction to a selection of her poems in the volume *Six Women Poets*, Nichols discusses what it is like to have to struggle to reclaim one's language, which is an indicator of identity.

Creole is to her the language that represents the struggle of slaves to claim a new tongue and thus an identity for themselves, after the loss of their original languages on the plantations.

In her case she seeks a fusion of Creole and Standard English because her background embraces both. She is aware that her identity, like Benjamin Zephaniah's (see page 77), is based on a mixture of cultures, and that being a woman and black can lead to stereotyping and thus a submerging of one's individuality.

3–5 **It's the battle with language... the challenge**   the imagery of battle here is suggestive of a struggle, intensified by *striving* and *challenge*.

6–9 **I tend to want... constantly interacting**   here she makes the link between language and identity.

12–14 **many Caribbean poets... are now exploring it**   the attempt to re-appropriate what was once one's own is a struggle common to many.

14–16 **a language our foremothers... losing their own languages** this makes clear that to gain a sense of identity through language was of fundamental importance to slaves. Having no language means having no voice, and hence no identity.

17 **a valid, vibrant language**   the alliteration draws attention to this key point. Creole is a legitimate language that is very much alive.

19–20 **We just don't see Creole as a dialect of English**   again this asserts the validity of Creole.

23 **As someone from the Caribbean**   Nichols noticeably does not describe herself as being of a particular nationality or race, but as *from the Caribbean*, thus not labelling herself and simultaneously asserting a sense of her individuality.

26–9 **I have a natural fear… we're all black**   here the choice of *fear* implies a positive aversion to being confined and labelled; *close in on me* suggests that being seen as having a group rather than an individual identity is suffocating; the repetition of *all* reinforces the notion of not being seen as having an individual identity.

35–7 **There is a great danger … 'sufferers'**   clearly Nichols is giving a warning about the restrictiveness of labelling and the dangers of not seeing people as individuals with separate identities.

Captain Corelli's Mandolin: Louis de Bernières (1994)

Louis de Bernières was born in London in 1954 and held a variety of jobs including landscape gardener before becoming a writer. As a teacher in Colombia his style was described as 'magic realist' and his first three novels show this South American influence. He was selected in 1993 as one of the '20 Best of Young British Novelists' in *Granta* magazine.

Captain Corelli's Mandolin is his fourth and most famous novel, and won the Commonwealth Writers Prize in 1995. His later novels include *Birds Without Wings*, which describes the lives of characters from *Captain Corelli's Mandolin* before the events of that text, and *A Partisan's Daughter* published in 2008.

Loius de Bernières claims that he writes his novels in separate freestanding chapters and then decides on the order in which he will present them only when he has finished them all.

The extract here is from Chapter 4, 'L'Omosessuale (1)', and is written in the voice of Carlo Guercio, one of the Italian soldiers who, with Antonio Corelli, forms part of the Italian occupation force on the Greek island of Cephallonia during the Second World War.

The fact that the chapter title is in Italian goes some way towards explaining its nature as a confession to be read only after his death. Its subject is his struggle to exist in a world which criminalizes homosexuality, so that he must keep his identity as *l'omosessuale* secret.

1 **I, Carlo Piero Guercio, write these words**   the formality of this opening, giving the writer's full name, suggests the writing of a formal document such as a will.

2 **after my death**   the seriousness of his intention is made clear.

3 **scorn... loss of reputation**   this indicates what Carlo fears should his true identity be revealed.

7–8 **condemned to wear the mask decreed by misfortune**   the emotive words *condemned* and *misfortune* imply that being homosexual is in his eyes like undergoing a prison sentence, and the result of fate.

9 **reduced to eternal and infinite silence**   this presents the idea that he can never reveal his true identity.

11–14 **that it is... have a choice**   this lengthy list shows how much experience Carlo has had so far of being advised not to be what he is. A similar list follows in the next paragraph, suggesting that there is no relief from this advice.

15 **I know in advance**   this repetition of the phrase used in the previous paragraph (lines 10–11) implies his weary familiarity with all that anyone might say about his being who and what he is.

20–1 **I must marry and lead the life of a normal man**   this is also repeated from the previous paragraph, as if this is the self-evident end of any advice. The phrase *normal man* implies that homosexuality is abnormal, hence his need to hide his identity.

22 **What could I say to such priests and doctors?**   Carlo's question here, in which *such priests and doctors* are presented as authorities to whom he might offer an explanation, is answered in the rational arguments that follow.

31 **And the priest will say**   Carlo's dramatizing of a possible conversation shows how sure he is of the response he will receive. The theological lines of argument which follow refer to God and the Devil.

40–1 **I would say… moulded me**   here he uses the language of nature and biology such as a doctor might employ, and once again presents the arguments he knows will be offered against him.

45 **the Casa Rosetta**   a brothel.

52–3 **There is a conspiracy… in different words**   here Carlo is depicting himself as a victim of a deliberate policy of exclusion.

54–5 **I am like a spy… secrecy**   this simile vividly creates a sense of the solitude Carlo feels.

55–7 **I am like someone … to utter it**   this intensifies the sense of isolation.

58–60 **I am like Atlas… blood**   this third, hyperbolic comparison sees Carlo as suffering forever under an unbearably heavy and oppressive weight.

61 **I am a plant suffocated**   Carlo's images of suffering shift from similes to metaphor as his feeling of desperation increases.

65–6 **I am a foreigner… detested as cancer**   this final trio of comparisons reaches a climax with each depicting Carlo as one who, while constituting a part of a nation, a race or a body, is paradoxically treated as other, an outsider, a disease.

66–7 **as purely flesh as any priest or doctor**   this final comparison completes the argument against these two representatives of society, and asserts more confidently his own sense of identity as pure, healthy and wholesome.

Little Red-Cap: Carol Ann Duffy (1999)

Carol Ann Duffy was born in Glasgow in 1955, but grew up in Stafford. She graduated from Liverpool University, and in 1977 embarked on a career as a playwright, later working as a freelance scriptwriter for television. However, it is for her poetry that she is best known, and it has won many literary awards. She is regarded as one of Britain's leading contemporary poets and was awarded a CBE in 2002.

Little Red-Cap is based on the fairy tale 'Little Red Riding Hood', and is the opening poem to Duffy's 1999 collection *The World's Wife*.

The most famous version of the story is based on a tale by the Brothers Grimm, in which the child, Little Red Riding Hood, is walking through the woods on her way to visit her sick grandmother and is spied by the wolf, who approaches her. On learning from her that she is heading to her grandmother's house, he gets there first and eats the grandmother. He lies in wait for the girl, disguised as her grandmother, and swallows her whole when she arrives. A hunter rescues her by cutting the wolf open, and Little Red Riding Hood and her grandmother emerge safe and sound.

The earliest known written version of the tale, by Charles Perrault in 1697, is rather more sinister and ends with the girl being eaten by the wolf. He presents a moral at the end:

> From this story one learns that children, especially young lasses... do very wrong to listen to strangers... it is not an unheard thing if the Wolf is thereby provided with his dinner... there is one kind with an amenable disposition... tame, obliging and gentle... Alas!.. these gentle wolves are of all such creatures the most dangerous!

Duffy subverts the original story. Instead of an innocent female victim, we see a girl who willingly associates with the wolf, benefits from his experience (particularly of literature) and when he is *greying*, chops him up and sets off alone.

1 **At childhood's end** this is presented as both a geographical location and a rite of passage for the 'I' of the poem. She is moving from the protection of *the houses* into a more dangerous world associated with the end of her childhood and the beginning of her life as a woman.

2 The list here might represent various possible stages in life – school, work, and old age, all of which Little Red-Cap by-passes.

3 How do you interpret this simile?

5 **the edge of the woods** unknown and dangerous territory.

6 **first clapped eyes on the wolf** the colloquial register implies casualness, while *first* suggests a sequence of associations.

7–8 **reading his verse... wolfy drawl** the wolf is presented as a cultured performer, augmented by the detail of *red wine staining his bearded jaw* (line 9).

9–10 **What big ears... teeth!** an echo of the dialogue of the original story.

11 **I made quite sure he spotted me** this makes clear that the persona of the poem is no victim. She wants his attention.

12 **sweet sixteen, never been, babe** this parodies the language of pop lyrics and emphasizes her youth and inexperience. **waif** this implies she is both lost, as in the cliché 'waif and stray', and youthfully slender.

16 **I crawled in his wake** she is subservient to the poet-wolf.

17–18 **my stockings... murder clues** the loss of her virginity is implied.

21 This suggests an ecstasy of sexual activity in which she is complicit.

22 Here the original tale is completely subverted. Fear has been replaced by love.

23 **I slid from between his heavy matted paws** no reference is made here to the teeth of the wolf. The detail is almost tender.

29–30 **Words, words... frantic, winged** the repetition and listing imply excitement. This is what she has craved as a girl and has experienced as a woman.

31–2 **it took... in the woods** the use of enjambement gives the effect of a great space of time passing.

34–5 **a greying wolf... year in, year out** this consolidates the idea of time passing and suggests her boredom. She has taken all she can and the wolf can give no more.

36 **I took an axe** she is proactive. These lines recall the original story of the wolf's killing. There is no need for rescue, because the speaker is self-sufficient.

39 **one chop, scrotum to throat** clinical in its exactness, this perhaps echoes Shakespeare's Macbeth, who 'unseamed' his opponent 'from the nave to the chaps'.

143

40 This recalls the original story, but the addition of *virgin* suggests a kind of purity being given back to the grandmother, a rite of passage in reverse.

42 This focuses us on the girl's – or rather woman's – independence. The reference to *flowers* echoes the old tale (she was picking them when the wolf first saw her). They might also be seen as celebratory. Her singing implies carelessness as well as joy, and being alone emphasizes her self-sufficiency.

Knowing Me: Benjamin Zephaniah (2001)

Benjamin Zephaniah was born in 1958 and grew up in Jamaica and Birmingham. In 1979 he moved to London, and his first poetry collection *Pen Rhythm* was published in 1980. Since them he has written more poetry, plays, fiction, screenplays, a radio play and poems for children. He has acted in television and film, and produced music recordings. He holds a number of honorary doctorates, and after the publication of *Too Black Too Strong* in 2001, from which this poem comes, he went on to produce *We Are Britain!* in celebration of cultural diversity in Britain (2002), and contributed verses to *Chambers Primary Rhyming Dictionary* in 2004.

Benjamin Zephaniah claims that he doesn't have an 'identity crisis' and does not wish to write to win awards. *Knowing Me* humorously makes use of this idea of positively *not* having an identity crisis in a poem written in a mixture of Standard English and Afro-Caribbean English. *I don't have an identity crisis* is used almost as a refrain, thus reinforcing its message.

1–2 Instantly the language of the Caribbean (*de experts*) is mixed with informal Standard English (*letting my side down*).

3 Using a word like *game* parodies the idea of being alienated, seeing it a pastime rather than as a serious state to be in.

4 This again is a parody of what a black Englishman is expected to feel about himself.

9   Repeated until it becomes almost absurd, this sentence summarizes the state of mind of the poet – he is *not* struggling to gain a sense of identity, contrary to expectations.

12–13   **officers of the law… to identify myself**   the first phrase parodies the way the police are sometimes identified in a formal register, thus creating a sense of 'official' identity. The second is a joke which plays with the idea of identifying oneself, as if one is unsure who one is – hence a *look into the mirror* (14) puts all to rights. Again there is no struggle.

19–20   These and the lines that follow poke fun at the idea of therapeutic methods of searching for one's identity, as well as counselling or aggressively manifesting outward signs of who one is.

26–8   This is a straightforward statement of the facts.

34–5   The mixture of nouns relating to body parts and varied geographical adjectives is absurdly humorous.

38–44   These lines continue the parody of the language and concerns of those who are preoccupied with the idea of a crisis in identity – or even of a struggle to find one. Repetition of *me* makes clear that the speaker is certainly aware of and at ease with himself.

43–4   The terms *diversity* and *politically aware* are examples of Zephaniah's lampooning of the language used by those such as the *Workshop Facilitator* (line 45; in itself a title or even an identity to be made fun of).

48   **I can recognise my shadow**   this takes the lampooning further, as if to do this one has to experience stages of struggling before the moment of awareness arrives.

54–5   The shift from proper nouns depicting nationality to those describing states of mind here suggests that these are seen to take on a life of their own, as if each can constitute an identity in itself, some of them not desirable.

57   This satirizes those who seek to help others whom they imagine are undergoing an identity crisis.

66   **wide awakers**   this term borrows the form of *go getters*.
for rising and shining   this takes the clichéd imperative 'rise and shine' and makes it a continuous process.

68   This line plays with *rave* as verb and noun.

69 The word-play on *justice* and *just* distinguishes between an
    imperfect system (which is inauthentic, only a *kind of justice*)
    and genuinely fair treatment.
72 Here the poet's identity is asserted as belonging to the present
    and associated with Britain.
73 This creates a sense of immediacy and of a firm presence in the
    here and now. There is no struggle and his identity is secure.
75 The poem ends with a reprise of the poet's message.

Spies: Michael Frayn (2002)

The playwright and novelist Michael Frayn was born in London
in 1933, and studied languages at first then changed to
philosophy at Cambridge. He became friends with fellow student
Alan Bennett and they began writing together.

Frayn's work after university was chiefly in the world of
journalism, and he wrote regularly for the *Manchester Guardian*
until 1968. He also began writing novels in the 1960s, including
the acclaimed *Towards the End of Morning* in 1967 and *Headlong*
in 1999.

Spies was published in 2002 and won the prize for Whitbread
Novel of the Year. This extract comes from the last chapter of
the text when the narrator, Stephen, reflects on the mistakes he
made as a child, one of which involved his friend Keith's mother,
on whom the boys had spied, thinking that she was a German
spy.

His other error is another one of mistaken identity, namely
his own. He eventually discovered that his father was a German
and a Jew and that in 1935, when his parents left Germany, he
was 'reborn' as an English child called Stephen Wheatley.

In the extract he reflects on his attempts to come to terms
with who he is now that he knows of his German roots. The
struggle to find his true identity is confused by the fact that he
feels that he cannot sort out *which is here and which is there*
(England or Germany).

The narrator as an adult addresses the reader (*you*, line 51) in quite a matter-of-fact way, which belies the difficulties he has encountered in trying to come to terms with who he is.

1–2 **There were many things that Keith had been wrong about** the narrator assesses his childhood perceptions from the point of view of adulthood.

4–6 **There was a German spy… it was me** this asserts his identity, of which at the time he was unaware, as German. He labels himself a spy because he and Keith during their friendship had spied on Keith's mother.

7 **Everything is… has changed** the narrator articulates the paradox that surrounds his sense of identity. It is both the same as it was and different from what it was.

8–10 **Stephen Wheatley… Stefan Weitzler** this further clarifies the narrator's change of identity. The child Stephen has over time become older and has also over time become Stefan, but within the narrative he has been tracing his own progress.

10–13 **That undersized… he was registered** the narrator make a third attempt at clarification for the reader. It is almost as if the struggle to make sense of who he is has not yet ceased.

15 **I was reborn as Stephen** this implies that the narrator had a second life and thus a second identity.

17–18 **my father became more English still** this implies that identity can shift.

23–6 **It's the longing… the displaced everywhere** again the narrator presents a paradox: he is pulled both away (from where he is) and simultaneously towards (where he came from). The fact that it is *terrible* and *torments* him shows how difficult the struggle to come to terms with who he is has proved to be.

27–30 **never really taken flight… a real job** this series of negatives implies a lack of fulfilment and a sense of incompleteness in his life in England.

39–41 **I had a bleak few months… my adolescence** further paradoxes are highlighted here. His real native language (German) is paradoxically taught to him as an adolescent as a second language, and the place he should call home has to be learned about again.

43 **Of my father's past scarcely a trace remained** this
effectively cuts away part of the narrator's identity – as his
father's past is his too.

43–8 **His parents... Bomber Command** here the matter-of-fact
tone masks the horror of what happened. *Uncle Peter, or...
Bomber Command* sums up the irony that the narrator's family
in Germany may have been bombed by Englishmen while he
himself and his father were living in England. *Peter* is the uncle
of his friend Keith.

55–6 **The story... once again somebody else's** this shows the
narrator's continued lack of certainty about who he is.

64–6 **And now, before... which is there** this reiterates the lack of
clarity about identity and belonging.

66–8 **my children... tend each week** this suggests that time is
moving on, a cycle is being repeated, and that the narrator will
never have space enough in his life to truly clarify who he is.

Late Spring: Owen Sheers (2005)

Born in 1974 in Fiji, Owen Sheers was brought up in Wales,
educated in a comprehensive in Abergavenny and went to New
College, Oxford. He has written for radio and television and as
well as poetry has published a non-fiction work *The Dust Diaries*,
a travel memoir set in Zimbabwe (2004), and a novel, *Resistance*,
in 2007.

Sheers's collection *Skirrid Hill*, from which this poem comes,
is his second poetry volume and was published in 2005. *Skirrid*
comes from the Welsh 'Ysgyrid', derived from 'Ysgariad',
meaning separation or divorce. The theme of separation is seen
in many of the poems in this collection: geographical divides
between areas, separation between the dead and the living, the
shift from childhood to adulthood, or divorce (literal or
metaphorical) in relationships.

This poem looks at a formative childhood experience on a
farm, as does Heaney's *The Early Purges* (page 41), and vividly
recreates the expertise of the narrator's grandfather (compare

Heaney's *Follower*, page 40) in castrating lambs. Work which prevents the development of the lambs, and removes their chance of reproducing, paradoxically happens in spring, a time of burgeoning new growth. Tail-docking, in a further paradox, is seen in terms of *a strange harvest*, again connecting the work with a sense of fertility. The last paradox is that depriving the lambs of the ability to be mature males (emasculating them) is what makes the boy in the poem feel that he is, momentarily at least, a man.

In this sense, the poem is about rites of passage from boyhood to manhood, as well as the emulation of an older member of the family whose genes he shares. For the lambs, the process is reversed.

1 This line might suggest that being man-like is not quite the same as actually being a man.

3 **castrate**   in this clinical and blunt term, the harsh consonants contrast with the softness of the word *lambs*. The enjambement of the first stanza gives a feeling of fluidity, of a job done naturally and with ease.

4–6 The harsh alliterative qualities of *picking*, *plastic* and *purpose* match the harshness of the job being done.

8–9 **turned one… to play it like a cello**   this gives the work a gentler aspect, as if the lamb is a finely tuned instrument ready for playing, rather than a living being about to be emasculated.

12 **like a man milking**   again this associates the action of castrating with gentle, natural and life-giving qualities.

13 This metaphor suggests value and fragility.

16 The child helps his grandfather, but is also strangely passive as if his involvement is limited (hence feeling *like a man*, rather than being a man, perhaps).

19 The matter-of-fact tone gives the effect of an everyday occurrence.

22 **tails scattered like catkins**   this natural image suggests that the tails had dropped of their own accord because the time was ripe.

24 **a strange harvest**   this image again links the tail-docking with a natural process.

> **seeds we'd sown**   this creates a feeling of the togetherness of
> the grandfather and grandson, reinforcing the ideas of the
> opening stanza.

Mr Pip: Lloyd Jones (2006)

Lloyd Jones was born in New Zealand in 1955. His novel *Mr Pip*
has as its introductory quotation: 'Characters migrate' (Umberto
Eco). Jones make use of a character from another writer's work,
Pip from Charles Dickens's *Great Expectations*, and transposes
Pip's nineteenth-century English identity into that of a
twentieth-century schoolteacher in the South Pacific.

The Dickens novel is the only text available to the little school
in Bougainville attended by the narrator, Matilda. It is a tropical
island where civil war is a background presence, and where self-
appointed teacher Mr Watts is the only white man. He regularly
reads to the class from *Great Expectations*.

When rebel forces on the island demand that he explain
himself to them, he is forced to assume the identity of Pip in
Dickens's novel, as he narrates stories to them nightly. He
interweaves details of his own personal life with Grace, his black
partner, with those of Dickens's character, so that his own
identity becomes blurred between fact and fiction.

In this extract, Mr Watts is narrating an account of the birth
of his daughter and what this means to him in terms of the
possibility of merging black and white, and of establishing a
sense of identification with his unknown ancestors. Mr Watts is
an orphan (like Pip in Dickens's novel) so has had no sense of
family identity until the birth of his child. Furthermore, because
the child is of mixed race, he moves on to consider his whiteness
in an exclusively black environment.

Not only does his description reveal how closely he looked at
his baby daughter, it also enables him to identify with his lost
past, his lost unknown parents. Pip in *Great Expectations*

imagines his dead parents as resembling the character of the writing on their tombstones; Mr Watts has nothing to go on until this defining moment when he sees his *dead parents emerge* in his baby's face.

Mr Watts's revelations about his emerging sense of who he is and about recapturing a lost identity strike a chord within Matilda, whose interior monologue forms the remainder of the extract.

Matilda's father is at present in the *white world* of Australia, a sort of reverse of Mr Watts, who is the white man in the black world of Bougainville. Her thoughts about her father lead her to try to replicate Mr Watts's experience, the better to establish a sense of her own identity. Touchingly she has no mirror in which to check on her facial features and dismisses *still pools* because of their lack of reflective detail. Instead she uses a finger-touch picture of her face to compare herself to her absent father.

Her conclusion that any trace of her father in her would not simply lie on the *surface of things* but might circulate *in the heart, or in the head wherever memory collects* takes the idea of seeking personal identity to a new and deeper level. It implies that identity is not just a sum of physical parts, but also has emotional and intangible qualities buried deeper than the skin, whether that skin is black or white.

1 **But he did… to share** the sentence fragment quickly creates the sense of a shared experience.

3–4 **no finer or more appropriate moment** this indicates that something special is to follow.

4–5 **He touched his collar button** this vivid detail, presented in a terse sentence, suggests a displacement activity as if Mr Watts is not quite ready to impart his information.

7–9 **My darling Grace… Sarah** when he does begin to speak, Mr Watts's first statement is quite long, and portentous in tone.

10–11 **it wasn't the usual… he had said** the implication is that this is a unique occasion, one on which the narrator, Matilda, is not required to give assistance.

14 **Everyone saw... deepened**   this one-sentence paragraph enhances the tension. *Everyone saw him swallow* implies an unusual nervousness in the speaker. How would you characterize the atmosphere presented here?

15–17 **He smiled... laugh too**   the repetition of the reference to smiles and laughter underlines the fact that Mr Watts feels secure with his audience. The sharing of incipient laughter makes the occasion not just one of sharing but of joy.

20–1 **By the way... black white**   the comment is almost an aside, suggesting a casualness to his view of race and colour.

21 **If you are the blaming kind**   this too is offered almost as an aside and asserts a tolerance of others' possible lack of tolerance.

22 **blame it on the horizon**   this perhaps implies that blaming is pointless, the horizon being untouchable and infinite, almost like God.

32–3 **an explorer seeing new territory for the first time**   this metaphor gives the sense of his awe and wonder at the experience of linking himself with his parents and his past.

33 **familiar geography**   this continues the imagery of exploration, with a reference to the mixture of heritage which Grace and he have created from themselves (their familiar facial features). How do you respond to Mr Watts's description of his baby's face?

35–6 **a new world**   this suggests wonder as well as the culmination of a great task, perhaps echoing Miranda's exclamation from Shakespeare's *The Tempest*: 'Oh brave new world, that has such people in it!'

47–50 **I traced... listening ears**   the words *eyes* and *ears* are repeated, emphasizing the detail of her exploration as she tries to replicate, in part, Mr Watts's experience.

57 **out there in the white world**   this refers to the fact that Matilda's father is in Australia, in a situation that mirrors Mr Watts's position as the sole white man in a black world.

Interpretations

Themes and ideas

In the following section, the 34 texts and extracts printed in this volume are discussed in groups to make it easier for you to formulate connections between them. It is important that you can make such connections and comparisons between texts and extracts, focusing on similarities and differences between different pieces of writing.

The struggle for identity might be defined in a variety of ways. It might be dependent on or connected with any of the following:

- rites of passage
- family and family relationships
- gender – being a woman, women's rights; being a man, manliness
- race
- the writer's identity – the struggle to place oneself in the world of literary endeavour.

All of the above themes and issues are discussed in the pages that follow, and the extracts are considered under these headings.

There are also other themes that you might want to think about, such as:

- work
- class
- politics.

In some extracts the idea of the struggle is clearly represented. In others there is little or no struggle, and in yet others the very idea is subverted by the writer's use of humour. However, whether obviously, subtly or obliquely, all of the extracts have a connection with the idea of the struggle for identity.

The loss of innocence and rites of passage

A key stage in any young life is the time when the innocent perspective of childhood is lost. Such a moment marks a rite of passage in an individual's life. Three of the most basic rites of passage are sometimes referred to jokingly as 'hatchings, matchings and dispatchings' (births, marriages and deaths). More generally, rites of passage mark a change in a life, a defining moment after which nothing will ever be the same again. An individual may struggle against such a change or may struggle towards it. Either way it is rarely a smooth process, even when conventionalized by such public rituals as baptism, a graduation ceremony, the wedding service or a funeral.

Events such as witnessing a death, one's first kiss or sexual encounter, becoming a teenager, and first identifying with others as they work (as in Owen Sheers's poem *Late Spring*) can all be defining moments.

The extracts we will be looking at here are:
- *The Early Purges*: Seamus Heaney
- *Late Spring*: Owen Sheers
- *Little Red-Cap*: Carol Ann Duffy
- *The Company of Wolves*: Angela Carter
- *The Go-Between*: L.P. Hartley
- *Nella Last's War*: eds Broad and Fleming

In *The Early Purges* Seamus Heaney looks at the idea of experiencing one's first death. The six-year-old narrator witnesses the drowning of kittens on a farm where they are deemed *pests*. The poem also looks at how adults seek to reassure children by trying to soften the blows of life, as Dan suggests it is *better for them* (the kittens) to be drowned than to live. Their struggle is short and leads only to a pathetic death.

The incident remains in the narrator's memory because it is the first of such events. The vividness of the recollection is captured in phrases such as *Soft paws scraping like mad* and *tiny din*, which emphasize the boy's awareness of the noises of the kittens as well as their diminutive size.

His struggle to come to terms with what he has seen, to be 'adult' about the killings, is assisted by the passage of time. Learning to suppress reactions of first fear and then sadness at this formative experience is interrupted by the resurfacing of fear when more animals are killed. His eventual accommodation, when he reaches adulthood, of the idea of drowning kittens and the deaths of a whole variety of farm animals, masks his sensitivity to it.

Activity

Consider the last two stanzas of *The Early Purges*. What do you think is the significance in the change of tone and language in these two stanzas?

Discussion

The brisk, matter-of-fact tone in *Still, living displaces false sentiments* suggests that as an adult one has to be realistic and unemotional about matters such as the killing of kittens. Such *sentiments* are for children to indulge in, and the adjective *false* implies that it is a misplaced indulgence.

The language becomes more abstract (such as *sentiments*) and complex, while the throw-away adjective *shrill* implies lack of sympathy, almost irritation on the part of the adult narrator.

He draws a comparison between himself and town people, who talk of *Prevention of cruelty*, in contrast to what happens on *well-run farms*. However, the tone of the last line suggests that the narrator is putting up a front of imperviousness to the suffering of animals, and that for him it has been a struggle to accommodate such events as part of his life in a farming community. Finally he assumes a false identity as a practical farmer, hiding the compassion he feels for the 'purged' animals.

Owen Sheers's poem, *Late Spring*, which like *The Early Purges* also has a farm setting, sees a young boy gaining experience in co-operation with rather than in opposition to an adult, his grandfather.

Activity

Compare and contrast the feelings and attitudes of the two boy narrators in *Late Spring* and *The Early Purges*.

Discussion

By contrast to the boy in Heaney's poem, the boy in *Late Spring* who witnesses the castration of spring lambs feels *like a man* by virtue of the experience. He admires his grandfather at his work and suggests that the experience assists rather than mars his development. There is no struggle here. The transition towards manliness seems natural. Ironically it is the act that robs the lambs of their identity as males that makes the narrator feel a sense of his own new identity as a man.

The ending of the poem is suggestive of fertility and life, in contrast to the ending of *The Early Purges*.

Duffy's *Little Red-Cap* takes as its subject the struggle of a female child to navigate a rite of passage into womanhood, and looks at the shift in identity from girl to woman. The girl's struggle to gain a sense of autonomy is, as in *Late Spring*, at the expense of another, this time the wolf. Unlike the original heroine of 'Little Red Riding Hood', this one deliberately courts the wolf – a reverse of the fairy tale's relationship – and emerges from the forest *alone* and *singing*. The suggestion is that she is happy to be so, because she has struggled against the wolf's patronage (he is a poet, she a novice who wants his expertise), she has gained her independence, and her identity as woman is secure. She has even liberated her own grandmother.

This idea of a woman being competent to make her own decisions is taken further in Henrik Ibsen's *A Doll's House*, where the main character, Nora, struggles to free herself from her husband's rule and takes a stand against society's norms by leaving him to make her own independent life.

The Company of Wolves by Angela Carter makes a useful comparison with *Little Red-Cap* as both are based on the same fairy tale.

A nineteenth-century engraving of 'Little Red Riding Hood' by
Gustave Doré shows a traditional view of the tale

Activity

What similarities and differences do you detect between Duffy's and
Carter's presentations of the heroine and the wolf and their
relationship in these two extracts?

Discussion

Carter's heroine, unlike Duffy's, not only struggles with the danger
present in the wolf who is *hairy on the inside* (and thus much more
likely to harm her because his outside is not unattractive), but finds
herself surrounded by a multitude of wolves, as in the story's title. Her
struggle is over when she and the wolf find mutual happiness, as

157

opposed to her being subjugated by him; in the case of Duffy's poem, the woman takes an axe to him and stitches him up, literally and metaphorically.

The ending of the Carter story, in contrast to Duffy's poem, sees the heroine *between the paws of the tender wolf*, no longer in danger and certainly *nobody's meat*. This is only after a struggle in which she undresses herself and then rips off the clothes of the wolf, unlike Duffy's narrator. Throwing the clothes into the fire seems a dangerous tactic but her confidence in her new sense of self, the passiveness of the wolf, and the dying down of the blizzard (which symbolizes her struggle) contribute to her success in becoming a woman in her own right – and remaining alive. When he speaks of eating her she defuses the moment by laughing, and her confidence saves her.

The struggle for supremacy ends when the wolf is appeased by *immaculate flesh* which she offers willingly, and when she lays *his fearful head on her lap*. Thus the struggle for her identity reaches a calm and satisfying conclusion alongside the wolf, whereas Little Red-Cap is solitary in her independence.

L.P. Hartley's *The Go-Between* provides a contrast with the confidence of both Duffy's and Carter's heroines. Leo, the young boy reaching his first teenage birthday – a significant rite of passage – noticeably lacks such confidence. His arrival at teenage years causes him to feel confused and misled by adults, and to feel disappointed in and dissatisfied with himself.

Activity

Consider what Leo says about *playing a part* in the second paragraph of the extract, and his reference to *pretence* later in the same paragraph.

Discussion

By *playing a part*, Leo seems to be suggesting that he has taken on the role of another person, has suppressed his real identity and assumed a false one, which has fooled others and himself. He refers to trying *to impress*, which is seen by his nurse as reprehensible. By contrast

ONCE UPON A TIME

A more modern look at the 'Little Red Riding Hood' story is depicted in this poster of 1939 designed by Kenneth Whitley

pretence implies still being oneself, maintaining one's identity intact, but indulging in the kind of 'make-believe' that is typical of childhood games. His nurse's stipulation that *you could say who you were, when challenged* makes the distinction clearer. In pretending there is no sense of the loss of identity. In playing a part, there is.

Activity

Consider how Leo's treatment by his nurse contrasts with that of *the grown-ups* at Brandham (where he is currently staying).

Discussion

While the nurse is clear about Leo not impersonating anyone else, or playing a part, the adults at Brandham seem positively to have colluded with Leo in his role-playing and have encouraged it. Making him feel as if he were a grown-up seems in his view to have eroded his identity and at the same time *had puffed* him *up.*

Nella Last's War presents a different take on identity. The narrator here is of course not a fictitious person and her references to the troubled family in this extract refer to real people in a real time (during the Second World War).

Here the rite of passage involves having one's first child, with the complication that because the mother is unmarried (another rite of passage not yet undertaken, as her partner is abroad because of the war), a conventional identity as wife-and-mother cannot be achieved.

Being a married woman at this time would confer status on the *adored daughter* of Nella's friend as well as respectability. To have a child while unmarried would make her the subject of moral disapproval. Having sex before marriage was so frowned upon that the young woman has hidden herself from society. She has isolated herself in the Lake District with her aunt because she is ashamed and feels disgraced. So intense is her sense of society's disapproval that she has become ill, is uninterested in her child, and is likely to die, the final rite of passage for any human being.

Activity

Compare this woman's attitude to sex outside of marriage to that of the two young women in *Little Red-Cap* and *The Company of Wolves*.

Discussion

Both Little Red-Cap and Carter's heroine willingly seek out their men/wolves with no thought of marriage. Both willingly give up their virginity – as we assume did the young woman to whom Nella Last makes reference. However, there the matter ends in Duffy's poem. The heroine emerges from the forest by herself, autonomous and liberated. The wolf is dead. In Carter's story the heroine almost challenges the wolf, colludes in their night of sexual passion and stays with him. His tenderness (as she *was nobody's meat*) is our lasting impression of him, along with seeing her acceptance of her new role as his lover. There is no suggestion that society might disapprove, or that she would be troubled if it did.

The family and family relationships

One crucial way in which we gain a sense of self, of who we are and where we belong, is from our family and the relationships within it. This particularly applies to the relationship between parents and children, and many writers in this and the last century have used it as the basis for all or part of their work.

Relevant works here are:
* *Follower*: Seamus Heaney
* *Spies*: Michael Frayn
* *This Be The Verse*: Philip Larkin
* *The Glass Menagerie*: Tennessee Williams
* *Nella Last's War*: eds Broad and Fleming

Heaney's *Follower* presents a father-son relationship in which as a child the narrator is literally his father's 'follower'; the poem depicts a boy who *stumbled* behind his father or was carried on his shoulders, wanting all the time to emulate him, to be as he was and to do what he did in so *expert* a fashion. The narrator is almost wistful when he recalls *All I ever did was follow*, as if somehow he was deficient.

Indeed by calling him *An expert* Heaney creates an identity for the father, one which the speaker hopes to occupy himself when he grows up. In short he wants to be like him but it is a struggle, which literally involves *stumbling*, *tripping*, *falling* and *Yapping*. These terms almost characterize the young boy as incompetent.

Activity

Consider the final stanza of *Follower*. What, in your view, is the significance of the last sentence?

Discussion

The idea of the father *stumbling* behind the narrator can be taken both literally and metaphorically. On a literal level the father is depicted as an older man who may be infirm and unsteady, hence is physically *stumbling*. Metaphorically, Heaney might be implying that the father is behind in the sense of forming a part of the narrator's past, as well as supporting him. The phrase *will not go away* then becomes an assertion of security. It is as if the father cannot be separated from the son. Their identities are interdependent. The boy's struggle to be like his father in this way is successful because his father is part of him and he is part of his father.

Activity

How might you compare the attitude to the son in *Follower* to that of the grandson in Sheers's *Late Spring*?

Discussion

One obvious difference is that while the son in *Follower* feels inadequate in comparison to his father, as if in his shadow and thus not having an independent identity, the grandson in *Late Spring* considers himself to be *like a man* when watching and helping his grandfather as he castrates the spring lambs. The fact that they work together cements a sense of identification with his grandfather, and when the boy walks the fields alone later, his reflection that the work was done together cements the idea that the two are a team sowing *seeds*. This detail can support more than one reading, as can the ending of *Follower*. While the lambs' tails have been cast as if they are *catkins*, and hence the *seeds* of something new, they have in another sense, as family-sown seeds, distributed their genes, so that the grandfather and grandson share an identity, that which comes from belonging to the same family.

The extract from Frayn's *Spies* takes a retrospective look at the struggle for a sense of who the narrator is, over time. In this way it can be compared to the approach of the poets in *The Early Purges* and *Late Spring*, both of which use a retrospective narrative voice. In the case of Heaney's poem and *Spies*, the narrator comes to an accommodation over time with a situation that is in some way unusual or uncomfortable.

In the *Spies* extract, Stephen realizes that he is not in fact who he used to be. He is now an old man, whereas most of the narrative features him as a child. He now characterizes himself treading *warily in the footsteps of his former self*. There is little in the way of a struggle, though the adverb *warily* implies the need for care.

But there has been another significant change in identity, as he is not Stephen but Stefan. Initially there was no struggle; he was simply 'reborn' as Stephen when his family left Germany in 1935 and moved to England. The shift to Englishness seems to have been painless, as one parent *was English* and the other *became more English still*.

The idea of a struggle for Stephen is embodied in the idea of *restlessness* arising from the paradoxical situation of both *longing to be elsewhere* and *longing to be home*. This two-way pull is uncomfortable and distressing. He refers to it as torment, as if it is almost a punishment.

His description of his unsatisfactory life in England after his parents' deaths, and his quest to find out more about his father, leads to a matter-of-fact cataloguing of the information he learned about his family history (lines 43–8).

What gives him his identity is no longer there. Learning the language of his homeland is a struggle, *And yet, and yet…* he has stayed there, as if there is a sense of belonging and of finding his real identity at last.

Activity

Do you detect any similarity between what Stephen/Stefan thinks of his 'story' in lines 55–8 and Leo's reflections on himself in the extract from *The Go-Between*?

Discussion

Interestingly, like Leo in *The Go-Between* he thinks of his story as *somebody else's*, similar to the way Leo feels he was behaving at Brandham. He also refers like Leo to the idea of adopting a role when he mentions playing *the loyal disciple* to his friend Keith.

Philip Larkin's *This Be The Verse* is by its very title suggestive of subversion, a technique employed by Carol Ann Duffy in *Little Red-Cap*. Whereas Duffy subverts the fairy tale 'Little Red Riding Hood', Larkin borrows from and indirectly subverts the Robert Louis Stevenson poem *Requiem*:

> Under the wide and starry sky,
> Dig the grave and let me lie.
> Glad did I live and gladly die,
> And I laid me down with a will.
>
> This be the verse you grave for me:
> 'Here he lies where he longed to be;
> Home is the sailor, home from sea,
> And the hunter home from the hill.'

Stevenson had in mind a happy homecoming in death, and there is a strong sense of identity. Larkin seeks to parody this with the narrative voice in his poem.

There is irony too as Larkin's words are a reminder for the reader of Exodus in the Bible's Old Testament, where the sins of the parents threaten their offspring:

> for I the Lord thy God am a jealous God, visiting the iniquity
> of the fathers upon the children unto the third and fourth
> generation of them that hate me.

Exodus 20:5

Larkin subverts the original threat from an all-powerful God by emphasizing the inadequacies of the more homely *mum and dad*.

He suggests that the shortcomings of *mum and dad* arise from the shortcomings of their own parents, and that the cycle is unbreakable because it is genetically predetermined that we shall all affect the next and subsequent generations in the same miserable ways, 'unto the third and fourth generation', as the Bible puts it. To struggle against this is futile.

In the last stanza, however, Larkin suggests that one should put up a struggle against what seems to be the inevitable: *Get out as early as you can*. His last line suggests that there is one way to be successful in putting a stop to the replication of identities handed down with misery from one generation to another: *don't have any kids yourself*.

In *The Glass Menagerie*, Tennessee Williams presents a strained mother/son relationship in which the son struggles to assert a sense of identity separate from his dominant mother. Amanda's refusal to engage with any of Tom's complaints about her treatment of him increases his sense of frustration, until according to the stage directions he is laughing *wildly*, she is *fairly screeching*, and both are *gesticulating*. This vividly represents in physical form the struggle that Tom is undergoing.

The key issue between them is that Amanda has *confiscated* the books of her adult son, Tom (including a D.H. Lawrence novel) by taking them back to the library. Clearly what he reads is part of who he is, and to have his choices overruled is to undermine his sense of identity.

This undermining is also shown in the pattern of the dialogue. It is significant that at the start of their exchange it is Amanda who interrupts Tom. Not allowing him to finish an utterance is a way of controlling him. However, by the climax of the scene it is Tom who is the more assertive.

Also significant are Williams's stage directions. The long italicized paragraph of stage description, which refers to the *overthrown* chair on the floor, like the previous stage directions about laughing and screeching, reveals the degree of physical struggle there has been between son and mother. Finally Tom goes out, another physical gesture showing how difficult his struggle to be himself – a writer and obviously also a reader – has become; he can only retain his integrity by leaving the home.

Activity

What comparisons and contrasts can you draw between the attitude of Tom in *The Glass Menagerie* and the narrative voices in *Follower, The Early Purges, Late Spring* and *This Be The Verse*?

Discussion

Comparing this extract to *Follower* or *Late Spring*, it is clear that there is no sense in which Tom wishes to emulate his mother, unlike the boy in *Late Spring* who helps his grandfather, or the boy in *Follower* who literally and metaphorically sees himself as being in his father's footsteps. In contrast the child in *The Early Purges* is presented as very unsure of what Dan Taggart is doing and his rationale for it, when Dan says *Sure isn't it better for them now?* in defence of the act of drowning the kittens.

A comparison that can be drawn with Larkin's *This Be The Verse* is that his gloomy observation *Man hands on misery to man* is strikingly exemplified in the scene between Tom and his mother.

Nella Last's War also focuses on issues connected with family and relationships. In the case of the *adored daughter* it seems that despite her mother's and her aunt's support, she has given up the struggle to be identified as a respectable woman, without any kind of fight. It seems that, if the role or identity of married woman is denied to her because the father of her child is abroad fighting in the war, she wants to have no identity at all. Her apathy is such that she prefers to be dead. The extract suggests that any struggle has been on the part of the *young soldier father*, whose letters have had no effect on her, despite the fact that they *would 'melt stone'*.

Being a woman

In a world in which the majority of literary texts have been written by men – though not necessarily about men – a modern concern has been to give women a voice and to approach writing from a female perspective. Clearly this is what Carol Ann Duffy is attempting in *The World's Wife*. Fortunately the time has passed in which women writers had to pretend to be males (Currer, Ellis and Acton Bell were the names under which the Brontë sisters' works were first published). However, there is still a sense in which to be female and to be of account does, for many, necessitate a struggle.

The texts and extracts we shall be looking at here are:

*   *Woman Work*: Maya Angelou
*   *The Handmaid's Tale*: Margaret Atwood
*   *Song of Lawino*: Okot p'Bitek
*   *The Prisoner*: Amiya Rao
*   *A Doll's House*: Henrik Ibsen
*   *The Female Eunuch*: Germaine Greer
*   *The House of Bernarda Alba*: Federico García Lorca

Woman Work is one of the poems in Maya Angelou's collection *And Still I Rise* that celebrates the spirit of women and their ability to overcome the mere drudgery of life. The list of tasks the woman has to attend to is representative of those common to most women. The inexorable nature of the work is emphasized by the repetition and by the fact that the first stanza is longer than the others. Its monotony is highlighted by the simple repetition of rhyming sounds. All the tasks are noticeably done for others; nothing she does is for herself. It is as if the woman is of no account. Her identity is subsumed by other people and the tasks she has to perform for them.

Activity

Why do you think the last four stanzas of *Woman Work* differ in form and subject matter from the long first stanza?

167

Discussion

The last four stanzas are different, to emphasize the change in tone and content. Here there is respite, which comes from the world of nature, depicted as comforting. It is shown cooling her brow, like a friend, enabling her to float to her rest, kissing her like a lover and promoting rest. It is, she says at the end, all she has of her own. In the natural world the woman (who might represent all women) can be aware of herself and who she is.

The *Handmaid's Tale* by Margaret Atwood presents the struggle to retain a sense of identity, and ultimately its loss, in a futuristic and clearly urban world far removed from the natural one of *Woman Work*. Whereas the narrative voice in Angelou's poem has too much work to do and is losing her sense of self under its load, the narrator of the extract from *The Handmaid's Tale* finds that her work, which defines her as an independent woman rather than oppressing her, is suddenly and inexplicably withdrawn. This builds up to a terrifying climax in which she sees men armed with machine guns in the corridor as she is dismissed along with her fellow workers – all women.

The extract deals with what should be a typical day in the life of a family, the *usual* events of which are disrupted one by one. The female narrator begins her day as wife, mother and worker. By the end of the extract her identity has been stripped from her as it has from all the women in her workplace.

The narrator struggles throughout the extract to establish what is *usual* in a series of situations that become increasingly worrying and unfamiliar. You might compare this with the list of tasks in *Woman Work*, which has the effect of making the narrator seem overloaded. Here the effect is the opposite – a stripping away of all that is familiar in the narrator's personal and professional life. With no bank card, no access to her account, and no work, the narrator has lost her identity in a series of swift and increasingly bewildering moves against which she cannot even begin to struggle.

In *The Handmaid's Tale*, Margaret Atwood writes about a woman's
struggle to retain a sense of identity

Song of Lawino presents an African Acholi village culture in
contrast to the urban world of *The Handmaid's Tale* or the
Caribbean context of *Woman Work*. Here the narrative voice of
Lawino is that of a woman who is being undermined in her role
as wife by her husband's choice of a westernized woman with
whom she must share her husband, a woman *Who speaks English*,
which Lawino does not.

Her identity as an Acholi woman is being undervalued by her
husband Ocol, who has been exposed to Western culture and is
now finding fault with her because she is true to her tribe. His
new love Clementine aspires to be like a white woman, changing
her features in a way that Lawino logs in minute and critical
detail.

Lawino identifies herself as *the old type* and Clementine as *a modern woman, the beautiful one*. However, Lawino is clearly unhappy despite her acceptance that Ocol will have more than one wife. Her displeasure is not that Ocol has taken a new woman, as this is traditional in her tribe. What distresses her is that Ocol now seems not to value her for who and what she is. Instead he now *rejects the old type* and values a black woman who *dusts powder on her face*, using *ash-dirt* in order to look white, and uses *nests of cotton wool* to enhance her *flattened, dried* breasts. Interestingly, it is Clementine the rival who seems to be struggling for an identity – one that is alien to her but which she feels will please Ocol, notwithstanding how absurd she might seem to others.

Lawino's final comments suggest that Clementine is also masquerading in the identity of a much younger woman, when she observes *How aged modern women/Pretend to be young girls*.

The Prisoner is an unusual poem in that it presents a Bengali woman's life partly through the words of a third-person narrator, who gives a voice to the sari she never wears. The sari has an existence of its own, but one that is totally dependent on its owner. The latter in turn finds her existence to be totally dependent on her (mostly) male relations.

The 'she' of the poem is variously referred to as *the daughter*, *his wife*, and *the busy housewife*, so that her identity is never her own. From the time she first hears the sari calling to her from the tin trunk where her mother put it away (and likewise never wore it) until her old age, her struggle is against the constraints of time and the mounting pressure of the work she has to do for others. By the end of the poem time has almost run out and she is *Alone in the darkening shadows*. Significantly, she is never given a name, so there is no sense of the sari's owner having an independent identity. Like Nora in *A Doll's House*, she is subordinated to her role, and like the 'I' of *Woman Work* her list of tasks seems unending. However, there is no escape as there is for Nora and no respite or refuge in nature as is the case in *Woman Work*.

One interesting aspect of the life of the woman in this poem is her subservience to her in-laws (she is *In the father-in-law's house under the eye of the mother-in-law queen*, with a multitude of *inquisitive in-laws*). Another is the lack of time she has with her husband, so that there is *no time to… know each other*. Even to her husband her true self is not revealed as she has to *cook food, serve guests, wash plates* and so on.

It is only the sari that communicates with her and gives her a sense of who she is, or what she might have been. However, the way in which it communicates becomes increasingly enfeebled. First it *says*, then it *pleads*, but its pleas turn to *sobs*, and finally it only *whispers* as if its life is expiring while it is ignored and unworn. There is a sense in which the lack of individual identity for the woman in the poem is paralleled by that of the sari – if it is unworn it may as well not exist. Similarly, if the woman does not have time for herself, she too may as well not exist as a person with her own identity. By the end of the poem, when the lives of the sari and the woman are both over, neither has been appreciated for their true potential. For the woman life is *only tears*. She has achieved nothing for herself, while the sari is *in tatters*, metaphorically echoing the fragmented state of the owner's identity.

The final scene of Ibsen's *A Doll's House*, between Nora and her husband Torvald, is set in the colder climate of Norway in the nineteenth, not the twentieth century. Nora's struggle for her identity as an independent woman comes at the end of a play in which she has been seen as complicit in being treated like a child. When she was younger she lived under her father's roof as *his doll child*, and then became her husband's *doll wife*. Her life has been play rather than reality. Her struggle to comprehend this and to free herself from the constraints of a false life with her husband will involve a great struggle in the male-dominated society to which she belongs. Her proposal to leave the doll's house and to educate herself so that she will be able to understand herself will involve standing *quite alone*, a daunting prospect in the time in which the play was written and performed.

Germaine Greer's *The Female Eunuch*, a non-fiction text, presents the struggle for female identity as doomed to failure for some because of behaviour encouraged in infancy. In this extract Greer makes a series of comparisons between the way female children and their male counterparts are treated by their mothers. While boys are allowed and even encouraged to *get out of their mother's way*, girls are not and are closely supervised. Furthermore Greer claims that they are introduced to a *menial role* and *household skills*, which reminds us of Angelou's poem *Woman Work* and its long list of such skills as floor-mopping, cooking, gardening, ironing and child care. Furthermore, while boys explore in groups or gangs, girls are isolated at home where they become fearful, guilt-ridden and learn to regard themselves as victims.

Activity

Can you see any points of comparison between what Greer says about young girls and the heroine of *The Company of Wolves*?

Discussion

It is interesting to compare what Greer writes with its subversion in *The Company of Wolves*, where the female protagonist declares that she is *nobody's meat*. She is not the wolf's victim but his partner. Greer's description of a girl being *accosted by a smiling stranger* echoes the situation in *The Company of Wolves* when the heroine meets the man who is *hairy on the inside* but presents an attractive and smiling exterior. But Greer's description of little girls who are too frightened to *scream or run away* is subverted in the Carter story as well as in Duffy's *Little Red-Cap*.

Activity

What connections can you see between what Greer is saying about girls' play and Nora's words to Torvald in the extract from *A Doll's House*?

Discussion

The reference by Greer to little girls at home *playing with dolls* vividly recalls Nora's words to her husband Torvald at the end of *A Doll's*

House, when she tells him that she has been his and her father's doll and has been playing in a doll's house rather than being an adult independent woman.

Near the end of the extract Greer comments that it is difficult for women to be seen as intellectuals, very much the idea that is put forward when Nora comments to Torvald that they have never before had *a serious conversation* nor *exchanged a word on any serious subject*. However, while Nora blames first her father and then her husband for how she has been treated, Greer firmly lays the blame on the mother.

Lorca's play *The House of Bernarda Alba*, rather than presenting a household of both male and female offspring as in Greer's imagined home, looks at a house (significantly not a home) where there are only daughters in the charge of their widowed mother. This house is exclusively female. There are no 'girls' here, as the youngest daughter is 20, the eldest 39. However, the control that Bernarda the mother exerts over her family goes way beyond that described by Greer in *The Female Eunuch*, in that no one is allowed out. There is to be no chance that any of her daughters associates with others in *groups and gangs* as boys do in Greer's description. Not only that, but there is to be no association with men, except for the eldest, Angustias, who is engaged to Pepe el Romano, a character who is never seen onstage in this female-dominated world.

In this extract the struggle of two of the daughters, Adela and Martirio, to gain freedom and personal fulfilment is presented in terms of the possibility of becoming Pepe's lover. Their identity as sisters and being blood relations is secondary to this, as is highlighted when Martirio claims *My blood's no longer yours, and even though I try to think of you as a sister, I see you as just another woman*. For her what defines her and her sister's identities has been destroyed in the effort to become at one with Pepe.

Adela in particular sees herself as Pepe's partner rather than Bernarda's daughter and Martirio's sister; she rejects the family home, saying *I can't stand this horrible house*, and plans to *go off alone*, echoing Nora in *A Doll's House*.

Activity

Given that both want to leave the house in which they have been living for some time, in what ways are Adela and Nora different?

Discussion

Unlike Nora, who is determined to be alone without her husband and children in order to learn about herself, Adela projects a future with Pepe, even though he may marry her sister Angustias. (This idea of sharing a man may remind you of *Song of Lawino*.) Whereas Nora wants to free herself from the influence of Torvald, her husband, Adela imagines herself as subject to Pepe's whim (*he'll come to see me whenever he wants, whenever he feels like it*) rather than being in control herself. So much does she relinquish her identity that she imagines Pepe as *master in this house* and herself being under his *command* instead, of course, of her mother's. Her statement *I'm his* stands out as a complete abnegation of her own identity.

Her breaking of Bernarda's cane has powerful symbolic resonance. It is as if she were destroying her mother's identity as ruler in the house. In fact Adela refers to it as *the tyrant's cane*. However, Bernarda's resourcefulness includes not only chasing after Pepe but also calling for her gun. This rapidly redefines her as the person with the power. It is also instrumental in precipitating a crisis, which results in Adela's suicide when she believes that Pepe is dead and thus that her life is over. If she cannot have him as her *master* and be *his*, she chooses to be no one's and nothing. There is no sense, as there is with Nora, that she can be a person in her own right, belonging to herself. Unlike Nora, whose life at the end of *A Doll's House* is just beginning afresh, Adela's life ends.

Moments after Adela's death Bernarda, determined to avoid *shame*, redefines her daughter's identity, powerfully stating three times that she *died a virgin*. This redefinition of Adela's identity seems as easy as that to her. Adding that her daughter's body is to be dressed *as though she were a virgin* makes clear that this new posthumous identity is assumed only for the benefit of the outside world. It will be a false identity.

Activity

Compare this last idea with those brought to light by Leo in *The Go-Between*.

Discussion

The idea of a false identity is in Leo's mind when he realizes that the adults he is staying with are imposing an identity on him, one with which he is uneasy. They address him as a *little man* and he does not like this. He compares it to pretending to be someone else but retaining his own identity as Leo. This he was able to do safely at home when he was with his nurse, who always wanted him to be Leo and not *another little boy*.

Activity

Compare Adela's and Bernarda's attitude to shame and disgrace at the loss of virginity as well as to the (supposed) loss of a lover, to that of the young mother in *Nella Last's War*.

Discussion

The young mother described by Nella Last is so overcome with shame that she hides herself away, not in her family house but in the home of an aunt in the Lake District, far removed from the society to which she belongs. Her sense of shame, of no longer being the person she used to be – a virgin – is overwhelming when she faces motherhood without the identity of wife-and-mother which would give her respectability. Her *apathy and fretting* and drifting into illness are caused by her feeling of shame. This young woman, unlike Adela, does not actively take her life but she almost wills herself to die.

You could also contrast Adela's attitude with that of the narrator in *Little Red-Cap* as well as with that of the heroine in *The Company of Wolves*, neither of whom is likely to submit to her lover as her *master*, any more than to a parent who wields a *tyrant's cane*.

Being a man

While it is true that a modern concern of writers has been to focus on the perspective of women and the struggle for identity in a male-dominated world, there is another important theme that looks at the world from a masculine perspective and in some cases examines what it is to be a man.

The extracts to be looked at under this heading are:

- *Things Fall Apart*: Chinua Achebe
- *All My Sons*: Arthur Miller
- *Captain Corelli's Mandolin*: Louis de Bernières
- *An Evil Cradling*: Brian Keenan
- *The Badness Within Him*: Susan Hill
- *I Know Why the Caged Bird Sings*: Maya Angelou

Things Fall Apart has as its hero Okonkwo, living in a tribal society like that of *Song of Lawino* where having more than one wife is the norm. Like the mother in *The House of Bernarda Alba* he *ruled his household with a heavy hand*. Okonkwo's struggle to be perceived as the one in charge is presented early in this extract. Paradoxically, his struggle is mostly against himself. His life is so dominated by fear that he needs to inspire fear in the members of his family, but his main fear *lay deep within himself* and is defined as *fear of himself, lest he should be found to resemble his father*.

Okonkwo's struggle is the reverse of that described in Seamus Heaney's poem *Follower*. Most of us, as in Heaney's poem, gain a sense of who we are from our parents, and try to emulate them to a certain extent. We may naturally 'follow', but we may also reject what we see in a parent, and there may be a struggle to gain a sense of self separate from them, as in *The Glass Menagerie*.

The idea that parents adversely affect their children's lives in either case is put strongly in Philip Larkin's *This Be The Verse*.

Okonkwo wants to be as different as possible from his father Unoka, whom he perceives as a failure and weak. His determination to be the opposite of his father begins in childhood when he *suffered when a playmate had told him that his father was agbala*, another name for a woman or powerless man. The struggle is clearly continuing because his own family are in fear of him, his *heavy hand* and *fiery temper*, both of which suggest – when we read that he was not cruel by nature – that he is engaged in a perpetual struggle.

Okonkwo's son Nwoye is described as feigning annoyance with *women and their troubles* and likewise feigning *that he no longer cared for women's stories* to please his father. In fact Nwoye's struggle is the opposite of as well as similar to Okonkwo's. Whereas Okonkwo's efforts have been to seem unlike his father, Nwoye wants to be seen to be like his father.

The idea of the son being the father's 'follower' is made clear when we read that Okonkwo *wanted Nwoye to grow into a tough young man capable of ruling his father's household* and expects that he will be able to *control* women and children, both signs of manliness.

His attempts to masculinize Nwoye extend to telling him *stories of violence and bloodshed* which Nwoye pretends to like, when in fact he prefers his mother's allegorical stories involving the natural world. How much of a struggle it is for Nwoye to pretend to like his father's stories is clear when we read that his mother's story of Earth and Sky *was the kind of story that Nwoye loved*. How much Okonkwo struggles to force his son to be like him is evident when we read that if he was pleased with Nwoye he *no longer rebuked him or beat him*.

Arthur Miller's *All My Sons* is clearly about a very different culture and a different time from *Things Fall Apart*, as it is set in post-Second World War America. Here the struggle for identity is seen in Chris. The problem is that Ann has been engaged to his brother Larry, now dead. Chris has fallen in love with her and wants them to marry, but is constrained by the fact that in the past she was Larry's girlfriend – as if this defines her identity – while he defines himself as *Larry's brother* rather than as a person in his own right.

However, in the main part of the extract Chris attempts to come to terms with a newer identity as a man *in command of a company* during the war where the fighting caused the loss of most of his men. His claim that *they killed themselves for each other* implies a total sacrifice of the self, the ultimate relinquishing of identity for the good of the *company*. He refers to this as *A kind of – responsibility. Man for man.*

In his analysis of himself and his personal identity he sees himself striving for the good of the many rather than the few. He identifies himself more as a socialist man than the capitalistic one he would need to be to work uncritically in his father's business. After his experiences in the war, working *with Dad, and that rat-race again* makes him feel ashamed. It is as if he feels that he has falsely resumed his pre-war identity as the son of a businessman, a man with no sense of a common purpose whose sole interest is in money, striving within a capitalist economy, and working within the confines of the family. This is an identity with which he now feels uneasy, so much so that he *didn't want to take any of it*, including Ann herself.

Activity

Is it possible to see similarities between the plight of Chris in *All My Sons* and that of Okonkwo in *Things Fall Apart*?

Discussion

Chris clearly does not want to emulate his father, because they no longer share the same values. In this way his struggle is like that of Okonkwo, to be unlike his father.

He now knows what he does want – Ann's love. Nevertheless, he is still struggling not to view himself as being like his father, nor as simply the brother of Larry. In short, Chris's struggle is to dissociate himself from both father and brother and take on the identity of an independent man in his own right.

Louis de Bernières' novel *Captain Corelli's Mandolin* is a post-modern text (see page 208) where the story is narrated in a series of voices. This extract is the first confessional monologue by Carlo, a soldier in the Italian army of occupation on the Greek island of Cephallonia during the Second World War. His homosexuality forces him, at a time when it was considered unnatural, to hide his true identity and assume *the mask decreed by misfortune*.

This idea of a false sexual identity recalls Adela in *The House of Bernarda Alba*, whose mother falsely claims that the young woman died a virgin, and also has links with *Nella Last's War*, not just because both texts are set during the Second World War, but because like the unnamed young mother in Nella's diary entry, Carlo feels that he would be the subject of *scorn* and *loss of reputation* if his real situation were known. In all three cases, society's condemnation of sexual activity outside marriage is feared.

While the title of the chapter clearly proclaims his identity, albeit in Italian, Carlo has been reduced to silence and is only able to communicate the nature of his identity in a written, not spoken, confession. Carlo expects his words to be read only after his death.

Activity

What is your response to Carlo's reference to *eternal and infinite silence*, and to what other texts might this be linked?

Discussion

Carlo's words are poignant and recalls the final words of *The House of Bernarda Alba*: *Silence, silence, I said. Silence!* You might also recall that the young woman in the extract from *Nella Last's War* has cut herself off from all communication, having no interest in her child nor in the *frantic loving letters* of its father.

Carlo speaks of being offered a choice to *lead the life of a normal man* by the chaplain and the doctor. The very phrasing of this suggests that it would be an act. He has tried to deny his homosexuality but his reaction to visiting the local brothel was that

179

he felt like a traitor. His emotive language makes clear the strength of his feelings and how much of a struggle this has been for him. This struggle is against his real identity, and *to appear normal* involves him in activities that cause him to feel loathing.

The difficulties involved in his struggle are made more evident by his analogies between himself and a spy with a secret, or the only person possessing a truth but who is forbidden to utter it. This again underlines the idea of silence, characterized by the fact that his confession will never be heard but only read posthumously.

His references to being like *a foreigner* and *an alien* also strike chords with the situation of Stephen/Stefan in Michael Frayn's *Spies*.

An Evil Cradling is a non-fiction account of its writer's abduction and imprisonment in Beirut, and presents a struggle to maintain a sense of self in the face of physical violence so great that Brian

Brian Keenan (left) with his fellow ex-hostage John McCarthy after their release

Keenan, the writer, entitles the chapter from which this extract is taken 'Rape'.

His description of his attacker as a violator is powerful and links with the notion of rape, but interestingly he refers to wanting *every trace of him and the air in which he stood sucked out of that cell*. Keenan wants his attacker's identity obliterated, because *His presence was being pushed down my throat*, almost as if Said, the aggressor, is taking over Keenan's identity in a tangible way.

His reference to *that personality I had insisted on maintaining for myself* implies that it may not be his real identity but one assumed – an idea we have come across before – to cope with the circumstances he is describing.

More unusually, he sees his identity subsumed by rage. So powerful is it that he feels it *gather up its force in me and move towards the moment when it would explode*, as if the rage has a life or identity of its own which overpowers his. Nevertheless, his anger diminishes and is replaced by a determination not to be humiliated. Perhaps this can be compared to the notion of shame or disgrace in other texts we have looked at.

Finally his reference to *a part of me they could never bind nor abuse nor take from me* is an assertion of a strong sense of identity. His reference to *a sense of self greater than me alone* conceptualizes the self as an additional identity, or a greater identity, one which is more than just himself.

Susan Hill's *The Badness Within Him* also presents in short story form the idea of a part of an identity, one that is almost separate and a thing apart. The references in the extract to *the badness within him* almost grant it a life of its own, one that is apart from Col, the protagonist.

You might like to consider this idea in relation to what Keenan says in *An Evil Cradling* about a part of himself that could never be taken away. However, in Col's case this part of himself is defined as *badness*, not a power for good.

Col's notion, as he watches his father in the sea and the rest of his family on the beach, that he and they *are separate people now* suggests that he is developing a sense of self which is separate from *ties of blood*. In fact, he considers that such ties *make no difference*. You might compare this notion of blood ties with what Martirio says to her sister Adela in the extract from *The House of Bernarda Alba*.

It is interesting that the realization that blood ties make no difference leads to fear, as if Col suddenly senses his aloneness. It is as if all that anchored his identity has gone. At this moment his father is drowning, so that one of the blood ties which have given him his identity is abruptly severed.

Col's reaction of going down on hands and knees to find a foothold implies that he almost literally loses his balance and comes close to losing himself on the cliff ledge. His reaction to seeing his father's body being brought to shore, standing in the shadow of the cliff shivering and apart from his family, suggests that the separation has become yet more real. He is now on his own.

The fact that Col has undergone a change from being a child whose identity was bound up with that of his family members to becoming an adult, with the power within himself which he had previously been only half aware of, provokes a kind of catharsis or emotional release: *he wept*.

The reference to *the long, hot summer* ending, and along with it his childhood, recalls Leo's experience in *The Go-Between*. The final tableau of Col standing beside the body of his father vividly creates the idea that he has now taken over as the adult male in the family – a new identity which will subsume the old one, though *the badness within him* remains.

Maya Angelou's *I Know Why the Caged Bird Sings* presents a different culture – that of black people in the southern states of America. Its narrative viewpoint is that of a child, who in a short anecdote raises the idea of pretence, of claiming an identity different from the one which is truly one's own.

The narrator sets out of the dilemma of her Uncle Willie, crippled since childhood, who could not usually *pretend that he wasn't crippled, nor could he deceive himself that people were not repelled by his defect*. However, for one brief period he manages to reverse this and to *pretend to himself and others that he wasn't lame*. In his borrowed or pretended persona he is discovered *standing erect behind the counter* of the family store; the narrator's surprise is indicated by her repetition of *Erect* as a one-word sentence. His pretence includes hiding his walking stick while he converses with two strangers who will never know the truth about him. He even claims that it is he who looks after his old mother and his brother's two children.

The narrator is silently complicit in this feigning and realizes it is important to him that the couple take home a picture in their minds of *a whole Mr Johnson*, a person who only exists for *one part of an afternoon*. She watches him *lurch from one side, bumping to the other* after the visitors have left, as he goes to retrieve his hidden cane, which attests to the physical struggle Uncle Willie has had to undergo to inhabit his temporary identity.

Maya Angelou's *I Know Why the Caged Bird Sings* is set in the southern states of America

---

Activity

This concept of pretence, feigning, putting on a different persona or adopting a different role is a feature of several of the texts and extracts in this volume. Which ones stand out significantly for you?

Discussion

Here are some ideas of characters, texts and extracts you might consider:

- Nwoye feigning an interest in his father's stories in *Things Fall Apart*
- Uncle Willie pretending not to be crippled in *I Know Why the Caged Bird Sings*
- Bernarda's pretence about Adela's virginity in *The House of Bernarda Alba*
- Carlo pretending to be a heterosexual man in *Captain Corelli's Mandolin*.

Racial identity

In the post-colonial world, black writers in particular have worked towards finding a voice separate from that of past colonial masters, as Grace Nichols comments in her Introduction to *Six Women Poets*. Some writers have sought to celebrate their race as a mean of establishing a strong sense of identity, while others focus on the idea that racial identity is not an issue, as is the case with Benjamin Zephaniah's *Knowing Me*.

The texts and extracts discussed in this section are:

- *I Coming Back*: Grace Nichols
- *Beloved*: Toni Morrison
- *The Color Purple*: Alice Walker
- *Knowing Me*: Benjamin Zephaniah
- *Mr Pip*: Lloyd Jones

I Coming Back by Grace Nichols is a poem that gives a voice to the previously silenced black slaves. Here the struggle in life is implicitly almost over. However, the female slave sees herself in the next life as *mistress* in opposition to the *Massa* who is in possession of the power now, in the world as it is at present.

Her new identity is one that grants her the ability to transform herself into *all that is evil* to plague her master, and the list of identities that follows (the howling dog, the ball of fire, the *skinless higue*, the *hiss in yuh ear*, the *prick in yuh skin*, the *bone in yuh throat* and the *laugh in yuh skull*) are all threats to his peace. The sheer number of identities she will assume means that he, who in life was her oppressor, will be vanquished. All the identities she plans to assume are potential irritants, which gradually become closer and more intimate, finishing inside the slave owner's head, the very seat of his identity.

Toni Morrison's *Beloved* also explores the identity of slaves in the US in the nineteenth century, this time after emancipation but before black ex-slaves had established a sense of their own identities. This extract is particularly concerned with the idea of names and naming. It also highlights again how a woman's identity can be bound up with that of her slave master, her employer or her husband.

It focuses on the discussion of the names given to Baby Suggs. Her identity has been defined by others – significantly all of them men, much like the woman in *The Prisoner* or Nora in *A Doll's House*. The fact that her name was seen by Mr Garner on a sales ticket defines her as a commodity, the name itself being the choice of her 'owner', hence it is an imposition of an identity as his property. Indeed she says of herself, when asked directly what she calls herself, *Nothing... I don't call myself nothing*, as if naming herself is not her right.

Her attempt to become her own person only extends as far as choosing to accept someone else's name rather than having it imposed on her – her husband's second name, 'Suggs' and his choice of first name, 'Baby'. At the time the text is set, women would naturally accept their husband's name when they married. By doing this (although paradoxically it is concealing her own identity beneath her husband's), Baby Suggs is struggling to assert an identity different from that which she was given as a slave.

Her meeting with the *Negro girl* shows the difference between Baby Suggs and the Bodwins' maid, for while the latter is 'Janey', clearly an imposed name, she is dignified by the title *Mrs Suggs* and is afforded some respect by being addressed as *ma'am*. When Baby Suggs says *I'm free*, we sense that this is an important indicator of identity. Baby Suggs has come a long way from the person defined by a sales ticket.

Activity

What in your view is ironic about Baby Suggs's various names?

Discussion

Her various identities as 'Jenny Whitlow', 'Baby' and ultimately 'Baby Suggs' are all imposed by men. Significantly, Janey addresses her as *ma'am* and *Mrs Suggs*, which signify respect. Sadly in her own eyes she is *Nothing*, but there is a sense that by the end of the conversation with Janey she feels some pride in her role as a free woman.

The Color Purple by Alice Walker, like *Beloved*, also features the importance of names and naming. Throughout the text the husband of Celie, the main character, is referred to as Mr_____. It was common for black men to be called 'Mr', to signify respect, by their perceived inferiors, women. Slave owners and white men in general were given the title 'Sir' by black men to indicate superiority. Meanwhile his son Harpo's new partner is called, somewhat disparagingly, 'Little Squeak'. Her respect for Celie is shown by referring to her as 'Miss Celie', rather than the less formal 'Celie'.

Activity

How might you compare this use of names and modes of address with the discussion of names in the extract from *Beloved*?

Discussion

You might want to compare this with Janey, a younger black woman and maid, calling Baby Suggs 'Mrs Suggs' as a mark of respect for an older (and free) woman in the extract from *Beloved*. In addition, recalling Mr Garner in *Beloved* and his questioning of Baby Suggs about her name, it is Celie here who suggests to Squeak that she should be called by her *real name*, which is Mary Agnes, so that *maybe he see you even when he trouble*. The suggestion here is that being known as 'Squeak' or even the diminutive form 'Little Squeak' diminishes her in other people's eyes. Similarly Mr Garner's comment *Mrs Baby Suggs ain't no name for a freed Negro* implies that he feels she should have a name – and thus an identity – which is appropriate to a freed woman's status.

Being referred to as 'Mr' grants Celie's husband status. More seriously, when Sofia's children are likened to *little buttons* by the mayor's wife (as if they were not animate) and are called *colored* by the mayor (as if defined by their skin), social forms of address are entirely dropped. These terms signal the perception of the mayor and his wife that Sofia's children are inferior, a group rather than individuals, and one distinguished by skin colour. Sofia herself is invited to *be my maid* as if this confers a privilege on her when in fact it reduces her identity to that of a servant with no name and an inferior status.

The struggle that ensues when she rejects this diminution of her own and her children's identities is not just verbal but physical. It results in her arrest, detention and a beating so severe that she loses the sight of one eye. Celie's description of her injuries, particularly *She swole from head to foot* and *She can't talk*, suggests that Sofia's identity has almost been obliterated.

Curiously, Sofia's new partner is only identified as 'the prizefighter', as if that encapsulates his identity. Ironically, although he has more physical power than anyone he is least able to use it.

Knowing Me, Benjamin Zephaniah's poem published in 2001 and very much located in the twenty-first century, takes a completely different stance on race or blackness from that found in *The Color Purple* or *Beloved*. The stance of the poem's persona is that being black in a mainly white society does not necessarily bring problems, and most certainly not *an identity crisis*, notwithstanding the opinions of *de experts*.

Unlike most of the other texts or extracts in this section, this poem is suffused with humour to subvert the concept of confusion about one's identity, in particular black identity. If there is a struggle here, it is a struggle against stereotyping. This is made clear in the first stanza with the references to *alienation* and frustration, implying the need for *counselling*, and in stanza 3 where he refuses to regard himself as *a victim of circumstance*. All of these ideas are rejected as possible elements of the persona's identity.

In addition, his emphasis is on the importance of the present, not *the rootless future* and not *going back in time* (as in *Beloved* and to an extent *The Color Purple*), and on being an individual – hence the repeated rejection of those who are allegedly *just like me*.

This is an assertion of his separateness and uniqueness. It is also a celebration of being racially eclectic, as he refers to his *Jamaican hand... Ethiopian heart... African heart*, comically juxtaposed to the reference to *my Brummie chest* and humorously compounded by the triple chant of *Aston Villa*, a quintessentially English team name. There is also a clever joke in stanza 2 on the idea of identifying oneself in an official context, when he takes the police officer's instruction literally, by checking that *What I see is me* in the mirror of his car. The idea of *poetic missions* is also confidently absurd, the word 'missions' lending a mock-heroic sense of military importance to poetry.

A similar joke based on a literal interpretation is used in stanza 5 with the reference to not feeling lost and not beginning to look for oneself until asked to do so by a social worker. The last stanza uses more subtle humour in puns on *rave*, *just* and *justice*.

This lightness of tone pervades the poem, but the voice of the poem is also exasperated in the penultimate stanza when he asserts that he is *sick of people asking me if I feel British or West Indian... Confused or Patriotic*, as if all of these capitalized identities have become labels with which to stereotype an individual.

Benjamin Zephaniah's *Knowing Me* humorously rejects the
idea of an identity crisis

The tone of the final stanza, *I am here and now, I am all that Britain
is about/I'm happening as we speak* asserts a refreshing self-confidence.

Lloyd Jones's *Mr Pip*, like *Knowing Me*, is a twenty-first
century text that has a different slant on issues of racial identity.
Here we see the only white man in a black community reflecting
(like the persona in *Knowing Me*) on the eclectic mixture of races
that can constitute an identity, as well as on the idea that one's
sense of self comes in part from one's parents. (Compare
Follower and *This Be The Verse*.)

The main character here, Mr Watts, also subverts conventional
notions about race. Having told his listeners of the birth of his
daughter, he states quite casually and dispassionately: *By the way,
this is how white turns mulatto and black white*. His statement sound
as matter-of-fact as if it were a comment on colours used in
painting. Telling those who disapprove to *blame it on the horizon*
removes any idea of human guilt in the mixing of races.

189

His experience of looking into his child's face is a defining one for him, giving him a sense of identity never before achieved. Being an orphan means never being able to determine whether there are resemblances between himself and his parents, but now with a child he is able to see his *dead parents emerge*. It is as if the face of the child is a mirror of his own identity in which he discerns his mother's and father's features.

Activity

What similarities are there between what the extract from *Mr Pip* says and the views of the persona in *Knowing Me* about racial mixtures?

Discussion

As in Zephaniah's poem, Mr Watts refers to race as if it usually consists of diverse elements – *Anglo-Welsh heritage in a coffee-coloured skin* in the case of his daughter. Also like Zephaniah, Lloyd Jones uses the idea of a mirror as giving back one's self in refection, so that one sees and is able to examine one's self as is never possible in any other circumstance.

The extract from *Mr Pip* ends with the more philosophical notion that identity is not just based on a collection of surface features but is also located *in the heart, or in the head wherever memory collects*. It is as if identity is the sum of both outward qualities and inner, less tangible ones, located deep within the self irrespective of skin colour.

Writing and being a writer

A common modern preoccupation of writers is the very business of their own work, the act of writing. Some writers have experimented by putting themselves into their own creations, others talk of their characters taking them over and asserting their own identity, and yet others marvel at the physical wonder of words appearing on a previously blank page. Some authors play with ideas about whether what is written constitutes truth or fiction, and what is the status of both of these concepts in relation to the writer.

The texts and extracts which will be considered here are:

- *The French Lieutenant's Woman*: John Fowles
- *The Thought-Fox*: Ted Hughes
- *Digging*: Seamus Heaney
- Introduction to *Six Women Poets*: Grace Nichols
- *Making History*: Brian Friel
- *The Joy of Writing*: Wislawa Szymborska

In *The French Lieutenant's Woman*, Fowles plays with his readers by using Chapter 13 to halt his narrative and engage with them, or even to toy with them. The fact that he does this suggests that in some ways he is imposing himself on the reader and asserting his identity in a way that does not happen in more traditional narratives.

Fowles very swiftly casts doubt on the integrity – and thus the identity – of his characters and of himself, and advances the notion (seen in other extracts) of pretence. His claim to have *pretended until now to know… characters' minds* in order to write in their voice, and to have merely pretended to be all-knowing, subverts our relationship with the characters and with the author, and denies the validity of his identity as creator.

These concerns are typical of post-modern literature, and Fowles alludes to this when he comments that assuming the vocabulary and voice of a character is *a convention universally accepted at the time* his story is set, that is, a convention of Victorian and earlier literature, rather than literature of the late twentieth century.

He compares himself to a man in the garden below his character Sarah's bedroom window, suggesting that he has inserted himself into his own narrative, and that he has an identity within the pages of his own story. To unfold Sarah's state of mind to the reader was his intention, but his comment that if she had seen him she would have turned and walked into the shadows implies that his will would have been ignored by his own creation; his identity would have been overridden and hers would have prevailed. However, his comment *But I am a novelist* is an assertion of his identity as the author and of his role as the person in control, and this is made clear when he concludes *I can follow her where I like.*

With his other character, Charles, Fowles suggests another identity independent of the creator. He speculates that the created world (and thus the characters who inhabit it) and the creator or novelist must be independent. Charles seems to have the ability to assert his own identity over that of the writer by disobeying him. His claim that the act of disobedience – not walking straight back to Lyme Regis – came from Charles, *not myself*, suggests Charles's *autonomy*. The struggle to assert oneself as the author, to be a creator like God, means allowing *other freedoms to exist* apart from one's own.

These complex concepts are linked with the idea that not one of us is in control of anyone else, not even of ourselves. Furthermore, Fowles writes, we undermine any fixed sense of our own identity by the way we treat our own past; we *dress it up… gild it or blacken it, censor it, tinker with it… fictionalize it* as a book of our own, our *romanced autobiography*. These ideas will be returned to when we look at Brian Friel's *Making History*.

In *The Thought-Fox*, Ted Hughes similarly focuses attention on the writer and his role in the writing of, in this case, a poem. Just as Fowles refers to himself in the first person, 'I', so does Hughes in his opening line. The essential idea here is that a writer is an almost passive vessel into which comes inspiration, and this enables a poem to be produced almost magically. The 'I' of the poem envisions himself alone with a blank page which, by the end of the poem *is printed* by means of the thought-fox, his inspiration, which is presented as having an identity separate from that of the writer. As the metaphorical fox (his inspiration) gains momentum (comes *Across clearings*), so his identity is subsumed by the ideas which it represents, so that almost without his knowing it the page before him is written upon.

Whereas in *The French Lieutenant's Woman* Fowles toys with post-modern ideas about the nature of the writer and his relationship with his characters, Hughes's idea of poetical inspiration is perhaps more conventional and allies itself with the idea of the Muse traditionally invoked to inspire the poet to write. Shakespeare in *Henry V* calls upon a 'Muse of Fire', and Wordsworth saw nature as providing his inspiration. Whereas Fowles refers to his characters as having minds of their own (albeit as part of his, the author's, mind) and steering the story in ways he did not fully intend, Hughes envisages inspiration as the driving force behind his poetry.

The key image of the poem is the thought-fox itself, inspiration in the form of a living wild creature which eventually *enters the dark hole of the head* – its den and the seat of the poet's creativity. This suggests that the inspiration is at first separate from, and then an integral part of, the poet's identity. As a writer, or more specifically as a poet, his identity is not complete until inspiration fills his head and simultaneously *The page is printed*. The pun on footprints and ink printing on a page highlights this relationship between inspiration and writer. By the quasi-magical act of printing, the poet has been visited by his Muse, which has almost taken him over.

Seamus Heaney's poem *Digging* takes a slightly different view. His concern, like Hughes's, is what goes on in the head of the writer. What is inside his head links him with his family – specifically his father and his grandfather, with whom he shares the family's history. By writing about them he is keeping their identity alive and a part of the present. More than that, he is establishing that his own identity exists because of them and their shared experiences, because they are of one family.

His key image of the spade/pen conveys the idea of writing being like digging; a writer can delve deeply into the past of his family and recreate them on the page. Whereas at one point he feels inadequate, commenting *But I've no spade to follow men like them*, his realization that his pen is to him what the spade is to them makes his identity as poet valid.

193

The poem emphasizes what it is to be a writer in a family of non-writers, and examines his role as a writer who is descended from farmers. Heaney once referred to being 'educated out of his tribe' or family group. Here he engages in a struggle to find a valid place for himself within his family and realizes that in another way he is digging as they did.

Activity
Compare Hughes's and Heaney's ideas on poetic inspiration.

Discussion
Whereas Hughes sees inspiration suddenly coming towards him and filling his head, taking over his identity, Heaney's reference to *living roots* awakening in his head implies that the material for his poetry is already there within himself. Furthermore while Hughes positions himself as a solitary figure writing by night, alone until visited by the thought-fox, Heaney envisages himself in relation to his family, writing at his desk while his father digs outside his window. Hughes's inspiration creeps up on him, gains momentum and suddenly puts itself onto the page; Heaney considers throughout the poem his father's and grandfather's skill at digging, and in an epiphanic moment at the end of the poem realizes that they are part of him, and that his writing is as a result of his own digging into his head, the repository of his family history. This will keep them alive and thus validates his own identity as different from, but closely related to, them.

Grace Nichols, in her Introduction to *Six Women Poets*, makes three key points about being a writer and poet; the first is specifically about language and personal identity, the second is about her place in her family and heritage, and the third is about resisting stereotyping as a woman and as a black woman.

Her fascination with language is seen in terms of a *battle*, a *striving* towards truly representing her *voice* as a writer and the challenge to *create something new*. The lexis here is telling; the terms *battle*, *striving* and *challenge* all indicate a struggle, which she specifically associates with trying to *fuse the two tongues* of English and Creole. These are the two languages she grew up with and so are integral to her ways of defining herself. If she has always used them both, then both should appear in her writing.

She sees her language heritage as another way of defining herself; the language of her *foremothers and forefathers* is preserved in the work of the poet. Her act of writing will keep the language alive on paper, just as Heaney's writing about his family will keep them alive.

Nichols's notion of fearing *anything that tries to close in on me* ties in with her resistance to attempts to stereotype her as a woman, as black or as a writer. The struggle to maintain a sense of personal integrity, to write about what she feels to be important, is keenly felt.

Activity

Compare Grace Nichols's views about stereotyping in this extract with those of Benjamin Zephaniah in *Knowing Me*.

Discussion

Both pieces refer to the fact that other people's expectations circumscribe the writers' identities in ways they try to resist. Clearly Zephaniah's reference to being accused of *letting my side down* implies criticism by some who feel that he should write about his 'side' (or family or racial group) in a way that they approve. His mention of *poets exorcising ghosts* might well refer to writing about slavery – which he may choose not to do. Similarly people's desire to label him as *British or West Indian,/ African or Black, Dark and Lonely, Confused or Patriotic* has to be resisted.

Likewise, Nichols reveals a disinclination to write about *the 'realities' of black women in this country*, quoting as examples *racial discrimination* and *bad housing*. This in her view is restrictive of free expression. Only to be viewed as a 'sufferer' is, in her opinion, limiting.

Brian Friel's *Making History* takes as one of its themes the idea of writing history as truth, and whether there is just one truth about anything or any person. In this extract Lombard is attempting to impose his 'truth' about O'Neill on O'Neill himself, who is resisting.

Lombard's 'truth' is that O'Neill was *the great Hugh O'Neill*, that his name *was a household name right across Europe* and that his *whole life* is to be celebrated. By contrast O'Neill's view is that *the whole life* must include all his identities; he lists what in his view is every identity he has ever inhabited: *The schemer, the leader, the liar, the statesman, the lecher, the patriot, the drunk, the soured, bitter émigré*. The identities here are the antithesis of all that is embodied in the notion of *a household name* or of being great.

The fact that O'Neill considers himself to be fighting a *battle*, indeed his *last battle*, is significant in that it implies he is seeing himself ironically as the chieftain he used to be, and as a person who uses the language of military leadership. The fact that he is *going to fight* and *going to win* against Lombard, a writer and historian, attests to the idea that he will struggle to ensure that it is his concept of his own identity that is presented to the readers of Lombard's book rather than Lombard's imposed one.

By its very title, Wislawa Szymborska's *The Joy of Writing* takes us away from any struggle. Instead it substitutes a woodland setting and a bounding doe, part of which is *borrowed from the truth*. The metaphors about writing include predatory letters and clauses and, in charge of the whole, a writer who is in a position of power and can *rule absolutely*, recalling Fowles's ideas on the author in *The French Lieutenant's Woman*.

Activity

In what ways can links be made between *The Joy of Writing* and other extracts in this section?

Discussion

Like Hughes's *The Thought-Fox*, Szymborska's poem has an animal image at its centre. However, unlike the thought-fox, which slowly manifests itself and is the poet's Muse, Szymborska's doe, the product of her poetic imagination, is already created when the poem starts. The author's contemplation of it and the questions it raises about the authorial identity are central. The doe has a life of her own as she *rustles* and *pricks up her ears*. However the repetition of the adjective *written* and details such as the phrases *across the page* and *beneath my fingertips* make clear that the doe is being controlled by the writer, and not the other way around as in *The Thought-Fox*.

You might notice, too, that the delicacy of Szymborska's imagery (*soft muzzle, Perched on four slim legs* and the idea that *boughs* sprout metaphorically *from the word 'woods'*) is reminiscent of lines in Hughes's poem, such as *Cold, delicately... A fox's nose touches twig, leaf*.

A link can also be made with Heaney's *Digging* in that Szymborska, like Heaney and indeed Hughes, envisions the blank page upon which the poet makes her or his mark or print.

Also, the notion of *the truth* is one that features significantly in Friel's *Making History* and in Fowles's *The French Lieutenant's Woman*. Like Fowles, Szymborska draws the distinction between text and reality, but unlike him her fictive world is one in which she claims absolute control, even over time, as *The twinkling of an eye will take as long as I say*. Although she does not explicitly claim, like Fowles, that the author is like God, it is implicit in such statements as *Not a thing will ever happen unless I say so*, and *I rule absolutely*, and even more so in *Without my blessing, not a leaf will fall*, since the word *blessing* is associated with religion. This idea of the author as a supreme being is clinched at the end of the poem when she refers to binding time and to making *An existence* like that of the doe *endless at my bidding*.

The final stanza of *The Joy of Writing* contains three phrases that sum up Szymborska's ideas. The first recapitulates the notion in the poem's title that writing is a joyful activity. The second suggests that it gives *power* to the author to keep and record things as they are. The third implies that writing allows *Revenge* on the real world where the author is not supreme, and where mortality takes its toll.

Language, structure and form

How a writer conveys his or her ideas is what distinguishes one writer from another. The methods a writer selects are part of the writer's toolkit, and though many techniques are shared, which choices a writer makes, how those choices are employed and what effects they produce are what make each author's work unique.

It is useful to consider aspects of style that are typical of the different genres – drama, poetry and prose – that we have considered, before narrowing down to the choices of particular writers.

Drama

Modern drama texts, unlike those of Shakespeare and his contemporaries, make extensive use of stage directions, some of which can be quite lengthy, to indicate the writer's view of how a character should behave, on the setting, the props that are needed and the dramatic effects such as lighting or sound that are required to convey meanings.

For example, Tennessee Williams's stage directions in the extract from *The Glass Menagerie* are relatively full and refer to details of staging such as lighting, sound and the arrangement of props and furniture. Stage directions also describe the ways in which the characters speak, and his use of exclamations, italics and capital letters also suggest increasing intensity and rising anger. The scene is of course structured to lead towards a climax of fury, culminating in Tom's exit. Their shouting implies that meaningful communication has almost ceased as Tom attempts to assert his individuality.

Arthur Miller, in the extract from *All My Sons*, lays more stress on how characters speak than on setting and props, but the clues about emotion are contained in stage directions next to the characters' speeches.

It is worth bearing in mind that such techniques replace what in a prose text might be called the authorial voice (or the voice of

Catherine McCormack as Nora Helmer in a 2008 production of
A Doll's House

a narrator), which can tell the reader whatever it wishes. However, some techniques are common to prose and drama, such as the specific dialogue characters are given. For example, the fact that the utterances of Chris and Ann in *All My Sons* are brief suggests the tension they are experiencing, and the use of ellipsis (leaving out words or leaving an utterance incomplete) implies their lack of confidence.

The use of stichomythia (a rapid exchange of dialogue in alternate lines) can suggest an increase in pace or urgency, as in the exchange between Nora and Helmer in *A Doll's House*. This dialogue is structured as a series of questions and answers so that a climax is reached in which Nora, like Tom in *The Glass Menagerie*, leaves.

The use of monologue (as with Chris's speech in *All My Sons* where he speaks uninterruptedly for some time) can reveal inner feelings perhaps as yet unvoiced, while the use of silence can intensify a dramatic moment. This is notable at the end of *The*

House of Bernarda Alba, where the simple repetition of the word *silence* emphasizes Bernarda's continuing oppression of her family and her decision to hide the truth about her daughter Adela.

A series of questions and answers can create tension, or suggest a character's incomprehension, or show a desire to assert the self, as in the dialogue between Nora and Helmer where he becomes increasingly perplexed and incredulous, all the time attempting to gain control of the discussion with his wife.

Leaving lines unfinished, as in the extract from *Making History*, can imply that one character is being interrupted by another in a struggle to impose one person's ideas at the expense of another's.

Having one character speaking the majority of the dialogue is another way in which a dramatist might suggest his or her dominance, while making a character remain silent will usually have the reverse effect.

Many of the above techniques could of course apply to the use of dialogue in a prose text.

Poetry

Samuel Taylor Coleridge memorably described poetry as 'the best words in the best order'. Compared to the language of most prose, the language of poetry is dense. Poetry can take a variety of forms; for example the sonnet is a tightly controlled form of poem in 14 lines with a particular rhyme scheme. Much modern poetry, however, is in the form of free verse, which means it does not conform to traditional forms and metres, although it does usually have rhythm and often rhyme.

Enjambement (where a line of poetry is not end-stopped by punctuation but the meaning runs on into the following line) and the caesura (a mid-line break or pause) are characteristic devices in many types of poetry, including free verse, which are used to reinforce meaning.

Most notably, poetry is characterized by the use of figurative language or tropes (similes, metaphors and personification) and rhetorical devices (such as alliteration, assonance, consonance and onomatopoeia). A poet's use of such devices is always meaningful and you need to consider what *effect* was intended when a simile, for example, is employed.

Similarly, the rhyme scheme chosen by the poet will be intended to help communicate the poem's ideas or subject. For example, the simple monosyllabic rhymes in *This Be The Verse* emphasize the force of the message and make the poem memorable. Heaney's rhyme scheme in *Follower*, however, is so unobtrusive as to be almost unnoticed on first reading, and complements the natural subject matter. Even more subtle is the rhyme scheme in *The Early Purges*, where the initial rhyming sound *drown* is echoed by *sound* in the same stanza and then repeated in the penultimate stanza to reinforce the idea of the returning fear the speaker describes when he sees animals being killed. The final sound *down* echoes *drown*, complementing the idea that the sound of drowning is one that echoes in the head of the poem's speaker over time, and that he is never free from the memory. The poem's structure, comprising two parts – one focusing on childhood and one on adulthood – is linked by this rhyming echo, suggesting that what happens in childhood affects the adult.

Sound can also be used in other rhetorical devices, and some of the most memorable yet simple examples of the use of alliteration, assonance, consonance and onomatopoeia can be found in Heaney's poem *Digging*, were the *curt cuts* of the edge of a spade dig into the soil and metaphorically dig through the speaker's head to reach his *living roots*. Here the repetition in the phrase *curt cuts* of the harsh, clean 'c' (alliteration) suggests the clipped sound the spade edge makes; the precise terminal 't' sounds (consonance) complement the precision of the cutting; and the 'u' sounds (assonance) link the two words together, suggesting the repetition of the movement of the spade. The onomatopoeic effect here is closely linked both to surface meaning (the act of digging is heard outside the window) and to the idea that the sound of digging into the ground awakens memories and reminds the speaker of *roots* or family bonds and heritage.

You might think that to describe the effects of these two monosyllabic words has taken a great many words on this page. That of course is the point; poetic language is extremely condensed, and all of the above would be registered in the mind of the reader as well as the writer, but to comment on its effectiveness requires many more words than used by the poet.

Prose

Like poetry, prose can take a variety of forms. Apart from the obvious distinction between fiction and non-fiction (such as *An Evil Cradling*), it may take the form of a novel, a short story (*The Badness Within Him*, *The Company of Wolves*), a diary (*Nella Last's War*, *The Handmaid's Tale*), letters (*The Color Purple*), a personal testament (Carlo's revelations in *Captain Corelli's Mandolin*), a first-person narrative (*The Go-Between*), a third-person narrative with an omniscient narrator (*Things Fall Apart*) or one with an unreliable narrator or an intrusive author (*The French Lieutenant's Woman*).

The form chosen by the writer will be significant. For example, a first-person narrative, while making the reader privy to the narrator's inner thoughts and feelings, gives a restricted view of other characters and allows the reader to make inferences about what the narrator does *not* say about himself/herself and others.

Figurative language and other rhetorical devices, of course, are as much part of the toolkit of the prose writer as they are of the poet.

Language choices and effects

Whatever you may notice about the way an author writes, you must always consider why he or she made such language choices, and what effects are achieved. In answering questions about a writer's choices, you might like to use expressions such as the following:

The use of the simile 'like…' gives the effect of…
The metaphor… suggests that…
When the writer uses… it implies that…

Remember the following structure for your writing:

Feature/device + quotation + comment/evaluation

This will ensure that your response is analytical rather than descriptive or explanatory.

Finally, since what we are considering here is *how* the struggle for identity is conveyed in modern literature, you might like to think about the following points.

- Some writers of the literature we have been considering choose to convey their ideas in an openly personal manner, often using the **first-person form** and in certain cases, for example *The French Lieutenant's Woman*, directly addressing the reader.

- A preoccupation with **names and modes of address** also characterizes literature on the theme of the individual's struggle to be recognized for who he or she is.

- Linked to this is another feature that more recent texts have in common – the tendency of writers to choose more **colloquial language**, the language of the spoken rather than the written word. Some use language that calls on alternative versions of English, such as the Creole used by Grace Nichols. Others use sexually explicit language or vulgar forms, as in Larkin's *This Be The Verse*.

- Some modern prose texts do not follow a conventional linear narrative structure, and may present a deliberately **fragmented narrative**. Writers try to transcend genre so that what happens (the plot) is subordinate to the way it is told (the narrative). It is, in short, as if the ways in which ideas about the struggle for identity are expressed suggest an intimacy between writer and reader, and a wish to dismantle any language and structures that might intrude.

Critical perspectives

In this section we will take a brief look at the major critical perspectives that have been significant in relation to modern literature on the theme of the struggle for identity.

Perhaps the most notable has been a **feminist** response to the writing and reading of texts. Issues of **race** and ethnicity are also highly significant, while the influence of **modernism** and **post-modernism** is important in the study of some of the texts in this volume. For some, a political reading such as a **Marxist** reading of a text, and to what extent it features the lives and concerns of ordinary working people, has featured prominently.

Feminism

The feminist movement is often thought to have included three waves:

- The first wave in the nineteenth and early twentieth centuries
- The second wave chiefly in the 1960s–1970s
- The third wave from the 1990s to the present day.

First-wave feminism of the late nineteenth and early twentieth centuries included the idea of the New Woman. This concept was a reaction to the cult of domesticity that characterized the Victorian era. The New Woman was educated, capable of earning her own living and politically aware. She was able to decide for herself who her partner might be and whether to have children. She was often depicted wearing more comfortable clothes and defying social norms to create a better world for women. Thomas Hardy's Sue Bridehead in *Jude The Obscure* and Bathsheba Everdene in *Far From the Madding Crowd* are arguably the most notable examples of the New Woman in the fiction of the time. *The Awakening* by Kate Chopin (1899) and *The Case of Rebellious Susan*, an 1894 play by Henry Arthur Jones, are further examples. Henrik Ibsen's *A*

Doll's House famously caused controversy for its presentation of Nora as a woman capable of handling the family finances (without her husband's knowledge) and finally becoming independent of him.

The women's suffrage movement focused on gaining votes for women and equal property rights. In E.M. Forster's *Howards End* (1910), Ruth Wilcox has the right to property ownership and bequeaths her home to Margaret Schlegel, a decision that is overruled by her husband Henry. However, it is Margaret who ultimately becomes the owner of *Howards End*.

Second-wave feminism concentrated on equality and sought the ending of discrimination through a variety of principles.

- *Bodily integrity and autonomy*, including rights to abortion, contraception and parental care, were key to feminists. In Margaret Atwood's *The Handmaid's Tale* this is undermined by the regime in Gilead, which takes away all of these rights, leaving women like Offred as a 'walking womb', subject to the rule of her Commander, enduring the monthly Ceremony and being consigned to The Colonies if she fails to reproduce.

- *Protection* from domestic violence, rape and sexual harassment is seen as a basic right for women. Interestingly, the Aunts in *The Handmaid's Tale* claim that the handmaids have gained 'freedom from' all of the above. This is in contrast with the rights enjoyed by 1960s feminists such as Offred's mother, which were prefaced by the words 'freedom to'.

- *Workplace rights*, such as equal pay and maternity leave, were also prized by second-wave feminists. One of the first signs of the repression of women in *The Handmaid's Tale* is the freezing of Offred's bank account, followed by her dismissal from work along with all other female colleagues.

Third-wave feminism was a reaction against the focus on educated, white middle-class women and led to the desire to find a space for black feminists. Writers such as Alice Walker refer to

'Womanism' as a movement which recognizes that black women might be subject to more intense discrimination than educated, middle-class white women. The position of poor black women is summed up by Mr_____ in *The Color Purple*, when he tells the main character Celie: *You black, you pore, you ugly, you a woman. Goddam, you nothing at all.*

Post-feminism has sought to see women as not being victims (as Celie was initially) and embraces a move against preferential treatment for women. This wave also includes 'difference feminists', who focus on the differences between the sexes in opposition to those who feel there are no inherent differences but that all disparities were due to social conditioning.

Race

Black writers have not exclusively written about black men or black women, but have taken a stand to give them space, and black characters a voice. In this respect the 'Womanism' mentioned above is significant in attempting to privilege Celie in *The Color Purple* and to celebrate the strength and independence of black women like Shug and Sofia. Less focused on black women as opposed to men, Toni Morrison's *Beloved* gives a voice to 'sixty million and more' slaves and highlights the struggle for identity in a world where names were imposed by slave owners and children often had little or no knowledge of their parents and forebears, and hence of who they were.

More recent black writers such as Benjamin Zephaniah in *Too Black Too Strong* have attempted to give a new perspective on the struggle and to assert an identity that is not defined by blackness. Zephaniah's poem *Knowing Me* playfully subverts ideas of identity crises and not knowing who or what one is. Likewise Grace Nichols wants to write about women, only some of whom are black. The notion of what it is to be black in a world that reserves privileges for whites is turned on its head in *Mr Pip*, Lloyd Jones's novel whose white protagonist lives on an exclusively black island.

Toni Morrison's *Beloved* gives a voice to those who suffered as slaves

Modernism

Modernism in literature, at its height in Europe between 1910 and 1920, sought to reject previous literary traditions rather than revising them. It particularly opposed the optimism of the Victorians, preferring pessimism, and focused on the quest for meaning and the alienation of the individual, as in Franz Kafka's *Metamorphosis* and Albert Camus' *The Outsider*. Works such as T.S. Eliot's *The Waste Land* rejected the cultivation of a central heroic figure typical of the Romantics, presenting instead flawed central characters. Jay Gatsby in F. Scott Fitzgerald's *The Great Gatsby* is one of a panoply of disjointed voices each claiming his or her own identity.

In addition, modernists developed new experimental forms such as the stream of consciousness seen in Virginia Woolf's *Mrs Dalloway* and James Joyce's *Ulysses*. They rejected what they saw as excessive or flowery language in earlier writers' works, using language that was sparser and was thought to mean precisely what it said on the page. Narrative flow might be disrupted and the narrator might be seen to be unreliable, as in *The Great Gatsby*.

Post-modernism

The term 'post-modern literature' refers to that which was written after the Second World War, and although there is no fixed date for its beginnings, 1941 – the year in which both Virginia Woolf and James Joyce died – is sometimes quoted as significant. Samuel Beckett's 1953 play *Waiting For Godot* marks for some the beginning of post-modernism.

Post-modern literature is characterized by experimentation in form, with fragmentation and unreliable narrators as in modernist literature. However, instead of the quest for meaning in a world of chaos, the post-modernist writer discounts the very possibility of meaning and parodies the idea of the quest, as in Gabriel García Márquez's *Love in the Time of Cholera*. The writer is undermined by the notion that it is chance rather than craft that is in control of his or her work – as in John Fowles's *The French Lieutenant's Woman* – and the work itself might be a parody or pastiche of an earlier work (as is Louis de Bernières' *Captain Corelli's Mandolin* in relation to Homer's *Odyssey*) or a reworking of an earlier piece, as is Angela Carter's *The Company of Wolves* in relation to *Grimm's Fairy Tales* or the work of Charles Perrault. Also of importance is the idea of playfulness with the reader, as in the extract from *The French Lieutenant's Woman* featured in this volume.

In some cases, the style and subject matter transcend the believable and become exaggerated or fantastical, as in some magic realist texts. Many of these have been written by South American writers such as Isabel Allende (*The House of the Spirits*) and Márquez, and are sometimes based on real characters as are Márquez's *One Hundred Years of Solitude* and *The General in His Labyrinth*. Likewise de Bernières in *Captain Corelli's Mandolin* incorporates fictional events into the lives of the real historical figures Mussolini and Metaxas, raising interesting questions about the integrity of identity. He also infuses Mandras's death with elements of the fantastical as he is brought onto land by his three (dolphin) friends.

Conclusion

These then are perhaps the most important critical perspectives relevant to the modern period and to literature concerned with the struggle for identity. A general appreciation of the critical context in which authors are working can be useful and illuminating as you read modern literature, helping you to appreciate familiar texts more fully and to discover new works on this fascinating theme.

Essay Questions

1 Read *Little Red-Cap* by Carol Ann Duffy. What view of childhood and the change to adulthood is presented here?
   - Compare and contrast the themes and ideas presented here with your wider reading. In your answer you might like to consider some or all of the following: the extract from *The Company of Wolves*, *The Early Purges*, *Late Spring* and the extract from *Nella Last's War*.
   - Compare and contrast how writers' choices of form, structure and language shape meanings.

2 Read *Woman Work* by Maya Angelou. What view of women is represented here?
   - Compare and contrast the ideas presented here with your wider reading. In your answer you might like to consider the extracts from *Song of Lawino*, *The House of Bernarda Alba* and *A Doll's House*.
   - Compare and contrast how writers' choices of form, structure and language shape meanings.

3 Read the extract from *Nella Last's War*. What view of the mother and daughter relationship is presented here?
   - Compare and contrast this with views of the parent–child relationship presented in other examples in your wider reading. You might like to consider some of the following: *Follower*, *This Be The Verse*, *The Glass Menagerie*.
   - Compare and contrast how writers' choices of form, structure and language shape meanings.

4 Look again at Philip Larkin's poem *This Be The Verse*. How is humour used here to present ideas about the struggle for identity?
   - Compare and contrast this with other extracts that use a form of humour to present ideas about the struggle for identity. You might like to start with the poem *Knowing Me*.

- Compare and contrast how writers' choices of form, structure and language shape meanings.

5 Look again at the extract from *The Handmaid's Tale*. Consider how the extract suggests that identity is informed by work.
   - Compare and contrast the ideas in this extract with others that consider the same idea. You might like to look at the extract from *The Glass Menagerie*, *Woman Work*, *The Early Purges* and *Late Spring*.
   - Compare and contrast how writers' choices of form, structure and language shape meanings.

6 Read the extract from Maya Angelou's *I Know Why the Caged Bird Sings*. Consider how the extract presents the idea of pretence or playing a role.
   - Compare and contrast the ideas here with other texts or extracts that consider the same idea. You might like to look at *The Go-Between*, *Things Fall Apart*, *Captain Corelli's Mandolin*, *The House of Bernarda Alba* and *Song of Lawino*.
   - Compare and contrast how writers' choices of form, structure and language shape meanings.

7 Look again at the extract from *Beloved* by Toni Morrison. Consider how the extract presents the idea of the importance of names and naming.
   - Compare and contrast the ideas about the topic in this extract with others that feature the same idea. You might like to begin with *The Color Purple* and *Spies*.
   - Compare and contrast how writers' choices of form, structure and language shape meanings.

8 Read the extract from Angela Carter's *The Company of Wolves*. Consider what view is given here of the development of girls and young women.
   - Compare this with other extracts or texts that deal with this topic. You might like to consider *The Female Eunuch*, *Little Red-Cap* and *The House of Bernarda Alba*.

- Compare and contrast how writers' choices of form, structure and language shape meanings.

9 Read the extract from Brian Keenan's *An Evil Cradling*. Consider what view is given here about issues of identity under circumstances of oppression, both physical and mental or psychological.
   - Compare this with the ways similar issues are highlighted in *A Doll's House*, *The Color Purple* and *Beloved*.
   - Compare and contrast how writers' choices of form, structure and language shape meanings.

10 Look again at Seamus Heaney's *Digging*. Consider what ideas are presented about the struggle for identity by the writer.
   - Compare Heaney's ideas with those in some or all of the following: *The Thought-Fox*, *The French Lieutenant's Woman*, *The Joy of Writing*, *Making History* and Nichols's Introduction to *Six Women Poets*.
   - Compare and contrast how writers' choices of form, structure and language shape meanings.

Chronology

Some important writers and significant works in relation to the struggle for identity in modern literature, other than those included in this book, are listed below. This list, which of course is not comprehensive, is arranged by the date of the author's birth.

Mary Shelley 1797–1851 *Frankenstein*
Anthony Trollope 1815–1882 *Can You Forgive Her?*
Thomas Hardy 1840–1928 *Far From the Madding Crowd, The Return of the Native, Jude The Obscure*
Oscar Wilde 1854–1900 *A Woman of No Importance, The Importance of Being Earnest*
Joseph Conrad 1857–1924 *Heart of Darkness*
Charlotte Perkins Gilman 1860–1935 *The Yellow Wallpaper*
Luigi Pirandello 1867–1936 *Six Characters in Search of an Author*
E.M. Forster 1879–1970 *Howards End, A Room With a View, Maurice*
Radclyffe Hall 1880–1943 *The Well of Loneliness*
Virginia Woolf 1882–1941 *Mrs Dalloway, To the Lighthouse*
James Joyce 1882–1941 *Ulysses, Dubliners, A Portrait of the Artist as a Young Man*
D.H. Lawrence 1885–1930 *Sons and Lovers, The Rainbow, Women in Love, Lady Chatterley's Lover*
T.S. Eliot 1888–1965 *The Waste Land*
Jean Rhys 1890–1979 *Wide Sargasso Sea*
F. Scott Fitzgerald 1896–1940 *The Great Gatsby*
Ernest Hemingway 1899–1961 *The Old Man and The Sea*
George Orwell 1903–1950 *Animal Farm, 1984*
Evelyn Waugh 1903–1966 *Decline and Fall, Brideshead Revisited*
Graham Greene 1904–1991 *Brighton Rock, Twenty-One Stories*
Samuel Beckett 1906–1989 *Waiting For Godot*
William Golding 1911–1993 *Rites of Passage, Lord of the Flies*
Lawrence Durrell 1912–1990 *The Alexandria Quartet*

Albert Camus 1913–1960 *The Outsider*
Anthony Burgess 1917–1993 *Inside Mr Enderby, Earthly Powers, A Clockwork Orange*
Muriel Spark 1918–2006 *The Prime of Miss Jean Brodie*
N.F. Simpson 1919– *A Resounding Tinkle*
J.D. Salinger 1919– *The Catcher in the Rye*
Iris Murdoch 1919–1999 *The Bell*
Paul Scott 1920–1978 *The Raj Quartet, Staying On, The Corrida at San Feliu*
Kingsley Amis 1922–1995 *Lucky Jim*
Elizabeth Jane Howard 1923– *After Julius*
John Fowles 1926–2005 *The French Lieutenant's Woman, The Magus*
Gabriel García Márquez 1927– *Chronicle of a Death Foretold, One Hundred Years of Solitude*
Jane Gardam 1928– *Old Filth*
Harold Pinter 1930– *The Caretaker*
Fay Weldon 1931– *The Life and Loves of a She-Devil, Wicked Women*
Sylvia Plath 1932–1963 *The Bell Jar, Ariel*
V.S. Naipaul 1932– *A House for Mr Biswas*
David Lodge 1935– *Changing Places*
Tom Stoppard 1937– *Rosencrantz and Guildenstern Are Dead*
Margaret Atwood 1939– *Alias Grace, Cat's Eye*
Angela Carter 1940–1992 *The Magic Toyshop*
Isabel Allende 1942– *The House of the Spirits*
Peter Carey 1943– *Oscar and Lucinda, My Life as a Fake*
Rose Tremain 1943– *Letter to Sister Benedicta, Sadler's Birthday, Restoration, Music and Silence, Sacred Country*
Michael Ondaatje 1943– *The English Patient*
Willy Russell 1947– *Educating Rita, Shirley Valentine*
Salman Rushdie 1947– *Midnight's Children, The Satanic Verses*
Liz Lochhead 1947– *Dreaming Frankenstein and Other Poems*
Ian McEwan 1948– *Enduring Love, Atonement, Saturday*
Peter Ackroyd 1949– *Hawksmoor*

Haruki Murakami 1949– *Sputnik Sweetheart, The Wind-Up Bird Chronicle, Norwegian Wood*
Martin Amis 1949– *London Fields, The Rachel Papers*
Laura Esquivel 1950– *Like Water For Chocolate*
Amy Tan 1952– *The Joy Luck Club*
Iain Banks 1954– *The Wasp Factory*
Louis de Bernieres 1954– *Birds Without Wings*
Kazuo Ishiguro 1954– *The Remains of The Day*
Jeanette Winterson 1959– *Oranges Are Not The Only Fruit*
Jasper Fforde 1961– *The Eyre Affair*
Yann Martel 1963– *Life of Pi*
Donna Tart 1963– *The Secret History*
Joanne Harris 1964– *Holy Fools, The Lollipop Shoes*
Helen Oyeyemi 1984– *The Icarus Girl*